Essays from the Heart

A Mother's Gift to Her Daughter

Essays from the Heart

A Mother's Gift to Her Daughter

Judith Kan

BookPartners
Wilsonville, Oregon

Library of Congress Cataloging-in-Publication Data

Kan, Judith, 1952–
  Essays from the heart : a mother's gift to her daughter / Judith
Kan.
    p. cm.
  ISBN 1-58151-061-6 (tradepaper)
  1. Young women--Conduct of life. 2. Chinese American
women--Conduct of life. 3. Mothers and daughters. I. Title.
HQ1229.K33   2000
  306.874'3--dc21
                                                          00-025509

Calligraphy by Judith Kan
Cover design by Richard Ferguson
Text design by Sheryl Mehary

BookPartners, Inc.
P. O. Box 922
Wilsonville, Oregon 97070

This book is dedicated to my children
Venus Killen
Amanda Killen
Nathan Killen
who show me life's splendor
with their love and inspiration.

Contents

Acknowledgments

To my parents, Henry Ying-Hong Kan and Mimi Kwok-Ching Kan, for their unconditional love and wonderful stories.

To my daughter Venus, whose coming of age inspired me to write this book. Her input is invaluable.

Special thanks to Darlene Flack, for her belief in my work. Her kindness and suggestions made all the difference during the writing of this book.

I am deeply grateful to family and friends for their support: Katherine Kan, Irene Sham, Norma Ng, Maria Kan-Lo, Eleanor Eng, Rod Politik, Kenneth Eng, Ronald Eng, Arloa Christiansen-Sambol, Diane Hansen, Jim Hansen, Paula Golden, Terry Golden, Dawna Robertson, Linda Sanker, Lisa Snella, Annette Young, Royce Young, Stephen Barkley, Bob Barrett, Catherine Kwong, Rosemarie French, Julie Owens, Sheri O'Sullivan, Evan Franulovich. Their feedback and encouragement mean the world to me.

Thanks to Ursula Bacon, my editor Joan Whitwood, Jini Gute, and everyone at BookPartners for their diligent work and publishing know-how.

As always, my deepest gratitude to my children: Venus, Amanda, and Nathan for their faith in me.

Part I

From Mother
To Daughter

A Letter to My Daughter

My dear daughter,

It does not seem long ago that you were an infant in my arms. To realize the miracle of life—you, my firstborn—bestowed on me, was absolutely overwhelming! I have fond memories of those quiet moments, feeling the warmth of your smooth skin and smelling that ever-so-sweet newborn baby scent. How quickly time flies! Today I am writing to you, my daughter, as you are about to embark on your journey into adulthood at the dawn of a new century and a new millennium. What an exciting time to come of age.

Very soon you will leave home for college. And with your departure, you'll be leaving your childhood behind. I have mixed emotions about this inevitable event. As a mother, I am proud of the woman you have become. And there is no doubt in my mind that you are ready to spread your wings and soar. So, why my sadness? I suppose, like most mothers, I am not quite ready for your childhood to end—and never will be. My memories of those precious years are compressed into fragmentary moments that will live forever in my heart. My goal as a mother has always been to equip my children with the skills to become happy adults, good human beings, and independent individuals so that the need for my parenting would diminish. And yet, I did so little to prepare myself emotionally for the moment of truth.

I have wanted to give you a gift that is unique. To commemorate your graduation day, I think it fitting to give you—in writing—my thoughts, some stories, and lessons I have learned from life. I invited relatives and friends who have enriched my life to contribute essays so you will have the benefit of their valuable insights, as well. All of these writings are my gift to you—my *Essays from the Heart*.

I believe life is about choices and consequences. Our life journey is composed of peaks and valleys. My hope is that you will derive some guidance from these essays for making choices in your own life—that from my failures and triumphs you will learn not to be afraid of making mistakes. This book is intended to heighten your awareness of your heritage—from your Chinese mother who comes from one of the most ancient cultures in human history, and from your American father who comes from the most advanced culture in the world.

I have great respect for individuality. I have always encouraged you and your siblings to be your own unique selves, and I still want you to be. If you find yourself pondering a problem and consult these essays because you want to know "what Mom would do," that alone will achieve my purpose in writing.

Aren't you glad I decided to compile all of my motherly advice to you in a book? You can always close me up and put me away when you have had enough of me, until the next time you need guidance or support.

I shall miss you! I shall miss your physical presence: your face, your voice, your smile, and even your occasional outbursts because you think I am in the wrong. I shall miss your opinions and friendly advice and the sound of your familiar footsteps marching up the stairs. Who else would leave an affectionate note on my night table saying, "For the love of God, Mom, please take me to the dentist while I still have teeth left!" Who will teach me all about the ska music that you like so much? Who will inspire me the way you did when you taught yourself how to publish a "'zine"? I think I can live without the insistent buzz of your alarm clock sounding long after you have left for school. But after you have gone off to college, what will I do during computer crises?

As you enter a new passage in your life, we, as mother and daughter, also enter one. The nature of our relationship is changing, maturing. You are going to live on your own, and I am happy to relinquish the role of your caregiver. I recognize that we are becoming less as mother and child, but more as advisors to each other. Do you know it is my long-cherished wish to share friendship with my children after they grow up?

I feel privileged to be your mother. You have taught me much about life. Try as I may, I know I am a far from perfect mother. Thank you for growing with me, my dear daughter. My heart is filled with gratitude that you have overlooked my shortcomings. I wish to tell you that I love you with all my heart and soul. The love between parent and child is both unconditional and eternal. It is because of you that I have come to appreciate one of the greatest loves known to humankind.

Do you remember the song from the children's book that we read many years ago?

> *I will love you forever,*
> *I will like you for always,*
> *As long as I am living,*
> *My baby you will be.*
> —Robert Munsch, *Love You Forever*

I am always, and forever will remain, your loving mother,

Mom

Learning

求學

Learning is like rowing a boat upstream.
If not moving forward, surely going backward.
                                                —Chinese proverb

During a recent phone conversation, my youngest sister told me that our father is the most important man in her life. "I have fond memories of the time I spent with Dad," she said.

When I think of my father, I think of his stories. My father is a great storyteller. I grew up hearing many stories about his life in China. His mischievous childhood, his boarding school experience, his young adulthood in Shanghai, and his eventual migration to Hong Kong—all were one big adventure to me. Over the years, I have heard the same tales many times over.

"You told me that before," I said to my father on one such occasion.

"Wait a minute, new details! Don't roll your eyes. You're going to miss them if you don't pay attention," my father replied.

Indeed, Dad had made an art of telling stories anew with different spices every time! Now, I realize that stories—recycled or not—are effective teaching tools. I learned much from my father's narratives during my childhood.

My father was born to privilege—the grandson of a peasant who made his fortune mining gold in Australia and became the big landlord of his village in Guangdong, a province in southern China. Throughout Dad's childhood he had a personal servant, a girl two years his senior who was sold to his family at a very young age because her own was too poor to raise her. My father's maid was raised as a slave until adulthood, when her owner arranged her marriage to a peasant in a nearby village. In old China, the future of a servant girl rested on the decisions made by her owner.

The nominal owner of my father's maid was my grandfather, but her actual owner was my grandmother. I know about my grandparents only through my father's stories. My grandparents were in an arranged marriage. My grandfather was frequently absent from his family in China. At a young age, he was sent to Australia for his education and also looked after the family import and export business. Every couple of years he returned to visit my grandmother, their daughter, and their four sons. Besides his family in China, my grandfather also had a family with an Australian woman: they had two Eurasian daughters. He lived most of his life in Australia and died in Sydney, long before I was born. I often wonder what life was like for a Chinese in Australia in a time of such racial prejudice.

My paternal grandmother was a "bound-feet" woman from an old bureaucratic family. In China, girls from well-to-do families had their feet bound, starting in young childhood, to prevent them from growing. It was considered the epitome of feminine beauty for a woman to have feet described as "three-inch golden lotus." As was customary in the old Chinese society, my grandmother, a daughter from a family with an illustrious past, was betrothed to my grandfather, a wealthy heir. She spent most of her life presiding over a family of children and servants, seeing her husband only during his infrequent visits from abroad. She died in Hong Kong when I was two years old. I would have liked to have known my grandmother, to hear her own account of her life— seemingly with so few personal choices—behind the closed doors of the family compound. The kind of life she led could easily have been mine if I had been born to my family only a few generations earlier.

As the turbulent political changes swept through China during the first half of the twentieth century, the lives of its people changed radically from the impact. By the end of the Chinese communist revolution in 1949, the Kan family fortune was reduced to a fraction of what it once was. All members of the family moved to Hong Kong to start new lives. My father successfully made the transition and raised a family, which I am part of. Some of his relatives were not so successful. I still have memories of one of them waiting at our apartment for my father's return so he could get some spending money.

"He didn't always live this way," said my father about his relative. "As a son of your great-grandfather's concubine, he had some money. What did he do with his money? He spent it all—traveling all over China with his concubine. He didn't have to work and never learned to work either. Laziness proved to be his undoing. His family really suffered." My father continued, "Be a responsible person—for yourself and your family. Never spend all your money. If you have a dollar, always save at least twenty cents." That was typical of my dad, always seizing an opportunity to tell us the moral of a story.

Looking at my father's family, I see that a fortune made can be a fortune lost. Nothing in life is guaranteed—not by birth, not by wealth. Life is unpredictable and full of trials. A privileged upbringing is not necessarily an advantage in combating adversity in life. Of my father and his three brothers, Dad is the only one who worked consistently. His brothers failed to work for a living. True, they did not need to work in China—the family fortune took care of their expenses. But when that fortune dwindled and work became necessary, they could not meet the challenge. What is the key to conquering adversity in life? I believe that a sense of optimism is important. My sisters and I nicknamed our father "Mr. Can" because of his "I can" attitude. His willpower and optimism were apparent when he had a cancer scare four years ago.

"What does it take to beat this?" my dad asked his doctor. Subsequently, he underwent two surgeries, one with major complications. He spent weeks in the hospital, including many days in intensive care. Fortunately, the tumor turned out to be benign. Throughout my father's ordeal, he never wavered in his belief that he could survive the battle. The right attitude is the answer to many challenges in life. In order to combat adversity, it is critical that we believe we can. The power comes from within.

When I was a child, my parents taught me about the importance of getting an education. The prospect of spending more than a decade and a half behind the walls of boring schools was not all appealing to me. Even with all the addition and subtraction skills that I had newly mastered, somehow I could not compute the logic of that length of time. Was so much schooling one of Confucius's ideas? If so, I certainly had no hope of winning an argument against the wisdom of the most renowned scholar in Chinese history. As a dutiful daughter, I did what I was told. It was not until years later that I truly appreciated the wisdom of this emphasis on education.

I was preparing to enter college in Canada, a foreign land half the world away from my birthplace.

Lacking direction regarding what to study, I browsed through college catalogs, hoping to get some ideas. I became keenly aware of the broad spectrum of classes offered in college curriculums. I could see that learning opportunities were far more abundant than in high school. Hadn't I been told that going to college would expand my horizons? The process of expansion began even before I set foot on my college campus.

In the years that followed, I attended classes, labored over homework and research, wrote papers, and studied for examinations. Earning my college diploma was hard work. Was all that effort a worthwhile endeavor? Yes! I have acquired an education in my quest for knowledge. Unlike material acquisitions, a college education is permanent—nobody has the power to take it away from me. I have found that the more I learn, the more there is to learn. There is so much to know, so much to be discovered. Interestingly enough, I did not unearth this revelation from textbooks or lectures. I became aware of it simply by being exposed to the learning environment of a college campus. My discovery reminded me of one of my father's stories.

"There was a frog who lived in a well. He thought that he was a wise old frog for he had seen everything in the world just by looking up to the opening of his well. One day he accidentally jumped out of his well. Lo and behold, he found himself under the boundless sky. Then he realized the extent of the real world—but only when he jumped out of his own little well."

Through higher education, I have come to appreciate the vast scope of the "real" world. I have chosen learning as an important part of my life's journey. Learning is a continuous process flowing like a river through life. A river without water is a river without life, and a life without learning is a life without living. Learning is not limited to time spent attending educational institutions. We learn from family, friends, and people whom do not know, from books we read, from stories we have heard or seen, and from our own experience and that of others. From learning comes an expansion of our mind, our vision, and our skills—the greatest vehicles we possess for connecting with our world.

The progress that we humans have achieved since the beginning of the twentieth century amazes me. Who would have dreamed, a hundred years ago, that information from around the world would be at our fingertips, accessible through the Internet? Or that surgery would be performed with a beam of light? I accredit our technological leaps and bounds partly to our ability to make good use of the knowledge that our civilizations have accumulated through history. All the inventions and discoveries of the past become the basis of new inventions and discoveries in the future. With today's technology, the rate of our progress will only accelerate. I cannot begin to imagine what the next hundred years will bring. As we enter the twenty-first century, I believe that higher education is more important than ever. College is a fundamental of basic education. I urge you to give yourself the advantage of a college career. It is a career of knowledge seeking. As in any other career, the basic elements for success are: hard work, dedication, and an inquisitive mind.

Continuing to learn throughout life is not always easy. I had always wanted to have a family sport so that I could play with my children even after they grew up. After my daughters learned to ski—at ages six and three respectively—skiing seemed like a good choice. I needed to drive them to the slope, and stayed for the day anyway. Standing in the cold watching from a distance while my children had fun made me itch to be part of the action. I longed to glide down the slopes with them. However, I feared falling and felt embarrassed to step onto the bunny slope at my relatively advanced age. The bunny slope was full of children! It took much internal persuasion for me to gather up the courage to take skiing lessons. Learning to ski turned out to be one humbling experience. I became an expert in getting up from falls. Those relentless falls bruised my pride more than my body. It seemed to take me forever to learn the skills that my children had mastered in a few short lessons. Thank goodness my children were not teenagers yet. Otherwise, they would surely have been convinced that Mom was stupid! After countless repetitions of "Good job, Mom" and buckets of frustrated tears, I finally descended the slopes with my family. It was not until the next skiing season that I graduated from the beginners' slope. Today, many years later, I hope that my children will play with me even after they have become adults.

Looking back at my skiing lessons, I congratulate myself for not quitting. Learning to ski was a challenge to my willpower. The challenges in life come in all different shapes and sizes. I met this challenge by sticking with the skiing lessons and eventually learning the sport. What motivated me? Although I had many moments of doubt about my decision to learn to ski, I could not possibly quit. I had always told my children that they could learn anything once they set their minds to it. How could I face them if I did not practice what I preached? By not quitting, I enabled myself to acquire a new skill—skiing—and to enjoy the pleasure of playing with my children. Persistence is a key factor in learning a new skill. It was years before I could ski with ease. Learning something well usually requires more than just instruction. It takes time and effort to master a new skill. Anything of value has a price. In the case of learning, the price is the time and effort we put in. The value is the skill itself, which enriches our lives.

I learned one hard reality of life long ago—people make mistakes. I certainly have, and I continue to make plenty of them. That is not to say I do not try to make good choices. On the contrary, I always try to exercise good judgment. In my naive youth, I often found myself wondering why I did not make better decisions. I shouldn't have been surprised. Considering all the decisions I had to make every day, it was inevitable that there would be some bad choices among the good ones.

Not long after I learned to drive, I mastered the art of making the tires squeal on turns. I took pleasure in the pizazz that added to my driving. While getting onto a freeway ramp one day, I realized that I needed to go over the recommended 25-mph speed limit on the curve in order to make the tires squeal. True to the heart of the young and the restless, I accelerated. Within a split second, the car was slipping out of my control. Panic! I stepped on the brake. My car scraped the curb and bounced back, making ear-piercing squeals. Fortunately, there was no other car close by. I drove on with my inexperienced heart pounding wildly. Knowing how lucky I was to have escaped an accident, I promised myself that I would never drive carelessly again. It took a near accident for me to acquire appropriate respect for driving. I made a mistake, but also learned a lesson. Driving needs to be taken seriously, because a moment of recklessness can have grave consequences. I have since become a responsible driver with a good driving record.

I believe that life is about choices and consequences. The choices we make dictate what happens in our lives—the consequences. It is certainly in our best interest to use our best judgment in the decision-making process, unless we delight in less than desirable outcomes. Even so, making mistakes is unavoidable. We need not be afraid of them. The important thing is to learn from our mistakes so as not to repeat them. Common wisdom is that the consequences of mistakes are usually unpleasant and sometimes painful. They need not be so. We choose how we react or respond to those consequences. We hold that power, nobody else. We can say to ourselves, "What is done is done. Let it be a lesson learned. I will not do it again…" and move on. Or, we can get angry at ourselves or others and let our anger ruin the day. That choice is ours to make. The attitude we assume determines how we view our mistakes. Taken with a sense of humor, mistakes can become great stories. Our friends love us for that.

My dear daughter, learning is a lifelong process. Commit yourself to learn continuously and as much as you can. Remember the importance of an education. Give the time and effort that are necessary to master a new skill. Adversity in life is meant to be conquered. Do not be afraid of mistakes and life's challenges. These are our life lessons that teach us wisdom. They are also elements that keep our lives interesting. Life without them would be boring indeed. Through learning comes our personal growth. Permit yourself to learn from life's challenges and the consequences of your mistakes. These, I promise, are worthwhile lessons.

文化的繼承

Heritage

Fallen leaves return to roots.
                    —Chinese proverb

I grew up in Hong Kong. It made all the difference. Hong Kong's population is predominantly Chinese, but there are marked distinctions between the culture of Hong Kong and that of China. This teeming, prosperous city was a capitalist state under British rule until 1997, while China was and still is a communist country.

Given the undeniable British influence in Hong Kong, as a child I found it natural that people often mixed English words with Chinese in conversation. American movies were mainstream entertainment. European fashion was trendy. Western food was not uncommon. Long before McDonald's invaded Asia, hamburgers, sandwiches, and coffee were standard menu items in Hong Kong's Western restaurants. When people refer to me as being from China, I often feel compelled to correct them.

From an early age I was aware of the differences between my family and those of many of my Chinese friends. Being a Christian family, we did not practice ancestor worship at home. I remember watching with fascination as my neighbors burned "hell money" and gold paper folded in the shape of nuggets for their ancestors to spend in the afterworld. As I watched the paper "money" and "gold" burst into flames, scattering ashes everywhere, I wondered if the ancestors would recognize their currency in the afterworld. The incense, the shrines, the porcelain figures of various gods—common in my friends' homes—were never present in mine.

My family always called me "Ju" or "Judy." I was given this English name along with my Chinese name at birth. Most of my friends in elementary school did not even have English names. It was common practice for students in Hong Kong to adopt English names in secondary school, but when they went home my friends were called by their Chinese names.

One day when I was in second grade, while walking to school I remembered that I had left my homework at home. Convinced that there was not enough time to go back and get it, I continued on despite my grave concern about the consequences. As we students, in a sea of white uniforms, were lining up for our daily assembly in the school yard, I heard a familiar voice calling out by the fence.

"Judy, Judy!" It was the voice of a neighbor boy. I did not respond to the call.

"Judy!" my neighbor shouted. I still ignored him, wishing he would just go away.

"Kan Ping Wing!" My neighbor called out my Chinese name. I turned to look at him. Seeing he had my homework in his hand, I realized that my mother must have asked him to bring it to me on his way to school. I immediately ran up to him.

"Why didn't you answer me?" he asked.

"I don't want you to call me Judy in front of everybody," I said.

I was embarrassed. My English name made good material for teasing. "Ju" has the same sound as "pig" in Chinese and I did not see pigs as particularly attractive creatures. If the other children had wanted to call me "angel" that would have been different. In my second grade mind, my sisters and I were the only people in the world who were burdened with English names. I did not want to be different from everyone else. My family was too westernized for my comfort.

As time went by, I realized that the Western influence in my family was rather limited. My family was Chinese at heart. Our home remedy for minor illnesses was "cool tea"—a steaming hot, bitter black herbal drink—a form of herbal medicine. Different varieties of the cool tea, each for treating different symptoms, were sold in the herb shops of Hong Kong. Whenever we had a common cold or fever my mother would cook a bowl of cool tea as the first treatment. The Western medical doctor came to visit only if the cool tea did not work. Drinking this boiling hot bitter tea was high on my list of "most unpleasant things to do." I usually needed a great deal of coaxing before drinking the bitter medicine.

"The cool tea and other home remedies are based on wisdom—thousands of years of cumulative knowledge on using herbs," my father explained to me on one such occasion. "Our home remedy tradition is as longstanding as our holidays."

My family celebrated most of the traditional Chinese holidays in accordance with the lunar calendar. Chinese New Year was my favorite and the biggest of all holidays with the great fanfare that accompanied it. I loved Chinese New Year because it meant vacation, new clothes, money, food, and merriment. As a child, I looked forward to the festivities and to my week-long vacation from school with no homework assignments. To welcome the beginning of the lunar New Year in style, like everyone else—adults and children—I was outfitted in my best new clothes and shoes. According to custom, we children would receive "lucky money" in festive red envelopes from married adults who were either related to or acquainted with the family. Little effort was required to earn the lucky money, except for a New Year's greeting. The Chinese New Year holidays were always the wealthiest time of the year for me. One of my favorite New Year rituals was counting the money I had "made" at the end of each day.

As in the Chinese family tradition, my mother began to prepare for the arrival of the lunar New Year weeks in advance, usually with a thorough house-cleaning known as the "big sweep," which symbolized sweeping out the bad things of the passing year. If you swept on New Year's day, however, you would sweep out the good, so nobody in my family touched the broom on that day. I was mystified by the double meaning of the "sweep"—same broom, same motion, magically transformed to mean the complete opposite by crossing the threshold of the new year.

"That's tradition," my mother said, "the sweep is nothing more than symbolic."

In the Chinese culture, rich in symbols and traditions, the plentiful, tantalizing dishes that families prepare for the holidays also have meaning. The menu of my family's annual New Year's Eve dinner was designed to symbolize wealth, prosperity, and everything good. We often had lotus root soup, for its name meant "have every year." The red color of the dried dates in the soup signified good luck. Chicken was served with head and feet intact to symbolize "beginning and end, thus whole and complete." Fish symbolized "remaining wealth," but the fish should not be turned over because that meant "sinking ship." The main vegetable dish contained Chinese mushrooms for "East and West success," dried black moss for "striking it rich," and dried oysters for "good things." When my family sat down to New Year's Eve dinner to conclude the passing year, my parents would announce the meanings and good wishes as they picked up the food. I knew for certain my wishes would come true the next day. The fortunate dishes would bring me wealth in the form of lucky money.

During the first two days of the new year, our home was buzzing with visitors, coming and going. Chinese New Year tradition dictates that friends and relatives call on each other to renew ties and to exchange greetings and good wishes. My family chose the first two days to receive visitors. While my parents were occupied with playing host, my sisters and I were busy collecting lucky money, playing with other children, and eating as we pleased. There was food everywhere—in the kitchen, on the counters and tables. Our dinner table, decorated with a vase of flowers on a red tablecloth—the color of celebration—was full of all sorts of tasty and symbolic festive foods: seeds, candies, fruits, cakes, and other New Year's goodies. As the adults drank their tea and nibbled on the food politely, we children gobbled up platefuls, helping after helping.

In accordance with my family's tradition, we started our visits to relatives and friends on the third day of the New Year. The first visit was to pay respect to my maternal grandfather, my only grandparent. The merry Chinese New Year celebration went on and on in the sweet aroma from continuous cooking of abundant delicacies, with streams of visitors, endless supplies of lucky money, and uninterrupted play. My family concluded the New Year festival with yet another luscious feast on Day 7, known as "Everybody's

Birthday." Then, with a box full of lucky money and a bellyful of indigestion, I started counting the days to the next Chinese New Year!

Much like the keepsakes in a treasure chest, the splendid New Year celebrations of long ago evoke warm feelings as I recall my childhood. Half a world away from Hong Kong and more than two and a half decades later, I still vividly remember the sights, sounds, and smells of Chinese New Year. Today I treasure my heritage, my culture, and my history. However, I did not always feel this way.

Soon after my immigration to Canada, I realized that my years of English lessons in Hong Kong were inadequate preparation for immersing myself in North American culture. We had a book discussion in my English class one day. Sitting in the reading circle, I could not utter a word even though I had read the book. I needed to perform a two-step translation process in my head before I could speak: first from English to Chinese to process the incoming information, then from Chinese to English to process the outgoing information. By the time I finished my internal translation it was too late to respond and I was too afraid to speak. Nobody knew about my problem. I was too shy and ashamed to speak of it. Sitting through class with the painful realization that there would be a lot of work ahead before I could integrate into my new country, I set my goal of overcoming the language difficulties.

Cultural differences proved to be yet another element I had to deal with. It took me a long time to feel comfortable accepting a compliment with a "thank you." In the Chinese culture, which encourages modesty, I was taught to deny a compliment. For instance, in Hong Kong when someone complimented me on my handwriting I would say no, the handwriting was bad or sloppy. Arguably, modern psychology could make a case about the effects of such negativism on my self-esteem. Did I think myself undeserving of praise? Certainly not. I was merely following the customs of my culture. Chinese culture considers humility a virtue. Agreeing with others' good opinions of me would appear to be boastful— and that would be impolite, as well.

During the formative years after I moved to North America I embraced the American way of life—with a wholehearted desire to be a part of the melting pot. My English improved as I spoke it more often, at home and with friends. I began to think and act more and more like my friends in my adopted country. My leisure reading materials shifted from mostly Chinese to primarily English. After my marriage to an American, the Chinese heritage that had once defined my life faded further into oblivion, like the last twilight of the setting sun, its once glorious rays soon to be a distant memory.

When I invite friends to my house for dinner, they are sometimes surprised that I do not serve

Chinese food. I often find myself explaining why I rarely cook Chinese dishes, although I love them. Never having learned to cook while living at home with my parents, I found Western cooking the easiest when I started to live on my own. I made more Western food than Chinese food because the preparation necessary in Chinese cooking—all the chopping, cutting and woking—is a time-consuming process for me. I would much rather use an oven than a wok, for there is less cleanup afterward. Why is it surprising when a Chinese woman does not cook Chinese? I suppose it is logical to assume that people will cook and eat the food they grew up with, especially delicious and popular Chinese food.

Similar thinking may be what prompts some people to ask me, "Where are you from?" With my accented English and Asian features, it is obvious that I am from somewhere else. Throughout the years of my conscious indifference to my background, I was reminded time after time that I wear my Chinese heritage on my face.

For many of those years, I raised my children according to American traditions, with little emphasis on their Chinese heritage. Typical native-born children of the United States, thinking, talking, and acting like their friends, my children identify themselves as Americans. They rarely mention their dual heritage. In our home, we have always spoken English. My children did not learn Chinese. They took a few lessons, but when their initial enthusiasm faded I did not make any effort to rekindle it. We celebrated American holidays. Chinese holidays were often forgotten. Although my parents sent lunar calendars to me almost yearly, I somehow managed to forget to use them.

For three to four weeks each year, my Eurasian children of American-Chinese parentage travel with me to visit my parents in Toronto, Canada, where we get acquainted with Chinese culture. Canada has fewer ethnic Chinese than the United States, but during their visits to Toronto my children hear their mother speak Chinese to her family, dine on Chinese food almost daily, and see how people in the Chinese community interact socially. As valuable as the visits to Toronto have been for my children, this is merely temporary cultural exposure, like foreign exchange students visiting a host country. My young children did not consider Chinese culture to be truly part of their heritage. By wandering off the path linked to my own heritage and culture, I unwittingly shortchanged my children on connecting to my half of their dual background. I hope to redeem myself in some small way by writing this book.

When my sisters and I were children my parents often began their instructions with the expression "The Chinese say...." For instance, we were taught not to put the mirror facing our beds because "The Chinese say that brings bad luck." In families of my generation, we did what we were told. We may not have liked it, but we did not verbalize that. I rarely raised questions about the validity of almighty sayings like "The Chinese say never sleep in wet hair." For years it made me uncomfortable to see my children going to bed with wet hair. I maintained that it had to be dry. When they were young they would usually comply. As they got older, however, they wanted to know the reason for my insistence on going to bed with dry hair.

"The Chinese say you'll get headaches if you sleep in wet hair," I said, remembering what my parents had told me.

"No, that's not true!" my daughters proclaimed.

"It's true. That's what my mother told me," I said, aware that my argument was flimsy.

"You don't know if that's true, do you?" my son asked, a grin spreading over his face.

Correct. I don't know. My parents convinced me that wet hair would somehow cause headaches. There was no need for scientific proof; I just bought it. Many years have passed since my parents last warned me about the dangers of going to bed with my hair wet, but I still act as if this theory were true. I have discovered that I still have "the Chinese" in me. My history stays with me; my heritage, my culture runs deep in my blood.

While heritage, culture, and tradition are immensely important to me, I do not find it necessary to follow all of my family's traditional practices. For example, I was never given vitamin supplements as a child. On the few occasions when I had all-important entrance examinations, my mother would prepare poached pig brain for me—to increase my brain power. The conventional Chinese belief is that animal organs provide good nutrition to the same organs in humans. Even though I disliked the notion of swallowing pigs' brains to energize my own, I understood that my mother meant well.

In the Chinese culture, the function of food goes far beyond fulfilling hunger. It is a key element in celebration, mourning, and social interaction. Chinese people prepare food for their family and friends as an expression of love, much like sending flowers in American society. As I looked at the pig brain in the serving bowl before me, I prayed that it would provide me with greater brain power than I saw in pigs. I have no intention of perpetuating this practice. If I discover a need to energize my children, vitamin pills will do quite nicely. I cherish the freedom to choose and retain only what suits me and my family.

As I grow older, I notice a longing to get in touch with my heritage and culture. This comes as a surprise to me. I feel more in tune with American culture than Chinese, I connect more easily with Americans than Chinese, and my friends are mostly Americans. Born and raised in a British colony, a naturalized Canadian citizen who has lived more years in the United States than in Hong Kong, never having set foot on Chinese soil—I want to reclaim the heritage of my origins. Didn't I call myself an international child?

One day a friend took me to our local Chinese cemetery. It was my first visit to such a cemetery outside Hong Kong. I was struck by the sight of rows and rows of tombstones inscribed with Chinese characters. Ethnic identity was obviously very important to families who had lived in North America, probably adopting Western ways. I have come to understand that although I can and do adapt, no matter where and how I live, my Chinese heritage is forever my identity.

Recently, I began to share some of the tales my father told me. I was delighted to find that my children were interested in these stories. Even my teenagers were eager to see the animated Disney movie *Mulan*, because they were already familiar with the Chinese legend. My older daughter says she intends to take Chinese as one of her college courses. Encouraged, I have begun to tell stories about my childhood experiences.

In 1997 I started a new tradition in my family: our own Chinese New Year celebration. There is a stark contrast between my version and the holidays of my childhood. Because of my underdeveloped Chinese cooking skills and a limited collection of recipes, I prepared a New Year's Eve dinner with only two symbolic dishes. A lonely festive tray with four different New Year's goodies—seeds, candies, candied fruits, and vegetables—graced my dining room table on New Year's Day. There were no New Year's goodwill visits because my original family and relatives are thousands of miles away. In spite of the humbleness of our celebration, my offspring seemed to be intrigued by this tradition. I detected smiles on their faces when I handed out lucky money. As I explained the customs and the symbolic meanings of the food to my children, I understood that I have come full circle in reaffirming and honoring my heritage. By being in touch with my roots, I have increased my children's awareness of their own dual heritage.

My dear daughter, this is a personal account of your mother's journey to come to terms with her heritage. May you always treasure your own unique heritage. You are a child of American and Chinese descent. Honor both cultures and their traditions, for they are the fabric of your being. That, I promise, will enrich your life.

Family

家
庭

Home is the one place in all this world
where hearts are sure of each other.
—Frederick W. Robertson

When someone inquires about my family, I often talk about my three children. The truth is I have two families. My family in Oregon is the one I created—myself and my three children. My family in my adopted hometown of Toronto is the one I came from—my parents and my sisters. Each family is dear to me in its own way, and brings to mind shared memories, love, and support.

I come from a family of five girls. With the first three daughters born within a three-year period, our home was not always harmonious. Sibling squabbles were a common occurrence. As the eldest daughter, I enjoyed certain advantages just by virtue of my birth position. When I was eight years old, my uncle selected me to accompany him and his children to a

Christmas dinner party at one of Hong Kong's four-star hotels—the British colony always celebrated Christmas. Our celebration at home, however, was a distant echo of Western Christmas. The novel sights and sounds of the hotel holiday festivities created wonder in my childlike mind.

"Look, a real Christmas tree!" I said to my cousin.

I had never seen a real Christmas tree until that evening, since we used an artificial one at home. I watched the dancing from the side of the ballroom, admiring the ladies in their glamorous evening gowns. Dazzled by the beautiful surroundings, I understood the magic of the Christmas season for the first time.

Back at home, my second sister—only sixteen months my junior—complained, "It's not fair! How come she got to go the ball and I didn't?"

Fairness was a major issue in my family when I was growing up. We were always fighting for equal time on the phone, dividing up the food, and taking turns using our only record player. When it came to chores, however, we graciously declined our fair shares. Today, my sisters and I delight in reminiscing about our childhood battles. We marvel at the wonderful friendship we share in adulthood. Growing up together taught my sisters and me important life skills. We learned how to compete, relate, fight, and make up. I often wonder if our childhood rivalry actually brought us closer together. We did all our fighting as children. With nothing left unresolved, we can relax and enjoy each other as adults.

Having four sisters also helped to expand my wardrobe. We were forever borrowing clothes from one another. My sisters are forgiving creatures. Even after some ferocious battles, we could always borrow a blouse or a dress. I never taught my daughters this trick of wardrobe expansion, but I have discovered that they do it anyway. My son also gets into the act. He exchanges anything but clothes with his sisters. Sharing comes naturally in a family.

My two teenage daughters occasionally have late-night conversations after their younger brother goes to bed. The faint sound of chatting and giggling brings back memories of my own childhood. My sisters and I used to share stories late at night, usually in whispers, over our parents' objections. Because space is at a premium in Hong Kong, we were living in tight quarters, and our conversations annoyed our parents. Although we were scolded repeatedly, challenging the authority of our parents was too tempting to resist and we carried on in spite of their objections. I did not realize at the time that our story-sharing was a form of sibling bonding.

My sisters and I now live in Canada, Hong Kong, and the United States. We keep in close contact by phone, e-mail, and occasional visits. Never mind that we were once keen competitors, my sisters and I are the best of friends, with shared childhood memories. They are the people I know best in the world—little wonder after all those years of fighting and sharing. When we had a reunion two years ago, now adults with children of our own, we still borrowed clothes from one another and shared stories late at night. Old habits die hard. Our bond is forever.

Siblings are ideal candidates for good friends. They share their personal and family history, grow up with the same values, understand each other's strengths and shortcomings, and tend to keep in touch. These are valuable attributes in friendship. If you do not already share friendship with your siblings, who have so much common ground with you, reach out to them. Give friendship a chance! Quite often in life, things happen because we make them happen.

One of my maternal grandmother's sisters got married in the 1920s. Her husband took her to Hawaii and she never returned to Chinese soil. She had thirteen children. After my great-aunt's death in the early 1960s, her children and their spouses, one by one, came to Hong Kong to establish relationships with their mother's original family. It was their mother's dying wish that her children would never forget their Chinese roots. I recall that communication was difficult in those early meetings with our relatives from Hawaii. They knew little Chinese and my family knew little English. But true to the common wisdom that where there is a will there is a way, we all managed to communicate somehow. As my English improved, I came to know some of my

Hawaiian relatives better. During my first visit to Honolulu in 1971, I met more than fifty members of my family, some of whom were of my generation. Even when I met these relatives for the first time, I felt a connection to them. I think of them as another branch of my family. We share common roots. More than seventy years after my grandmother and her sister found themselves separated by the Pacific Ocean, their descendants—my relatives in Hawaii and I—still maintain ties. Family connections transcend time and distance.

When I was a child, my father worked long hours. He came home early in the evening to have dinner with us and we would not see him again until late at night. Strangely enough, although I spent little time with him, my childhood memory is full of his presence. My father is a communicator. He told us stories and gave us his opinions on events in the community and world affairs. Through his stories, I learned much about him, our family history, his values, and the world around me. The time he spent with us, however short it may have seemed, left a strong imprint in my memory. Growing up, I always felt closer to my father than to my mother.

Ten years ago, when my mother came to visit me, I asked about some elective surgery that she was planning to have after her return to Toronto.

"Are you afraid?" I asked.

"No, I'm not afraid of anything—not even death," my mother said. "I've had a good life. I'm at peace with myself. Should I die during surgery, I want you to know I wish to be cremated and my ashes scattered at sea."

She spoke with such calmness, I was in awe of her. How could she face the subject of death with such serenity? I knew I couldn't. Death is not a subject I like to think about. The truth is, I am afraid of it. What would happen to my children if I were gone? Who would take care of them?

My mother said to me, "We are in different stages of life. I have completed my job of raising children. You all turned out well. I have no worries. For you—your children are young—there is still a lot for you to do. Death is an inevitable end of living. What good is it to be afraid? It is when we come to accept the inevitable that we can have peace within ourselves. Besides, I know I'll be fine. I know where I'm going—to God, my maker."

My mother and I had a long conversation that day, on many different subjects. It was then that I discovered my mother is a woman with more wisdom than I had ever given her credit for. How could I not have known her before?

Throughout my childhood, I saw my mother as a disciplinarian. My sisters and I seemed to get ourselves in trouble with her frequently. I did not feel close to my mother. We rarely spent time alone together. It seemed to me that she was always busy. Unlike my father, the storyteller, my mother is a listener. She is candid about her feelings when asked, but generally does not offer to reveal herself. I knew little about my mother's life before my existence, except that she was once a schoolteacher.

During the Japanese occupation of Hong Kong in World War II, my mother and her family escaped to their ancestral home in China. There, as a young adult, my mother became the village schoolteacher. Her salary was paid in bags of rice. Apparently, my mother's family lived reasonably well under that arrangement. Mother's work brought in the rice, and the rest of the family raised vegetables and livestock on their land. Nobody in my mother's family went hungry during their four-year stay in China—they survived the war by taking care of each other. Cooperation, support, loyalty, and comradeship are innate elements of family.

In raising her daughters, my mother emphasized being gracious and ladylike. One day when I was eleven years old, I came home red-faced after playing tag with the neighborhood children. My mother informed me that from that day onward, I would not go out and run around like a wild bird. I needed to start behaving like a lady, not all breathless and red-faced. Although I did not like my mother's idea, I did not argue with her. In the Chinese culture, we were taught to respect our elders. I would not dare to answer back to my parents. Instead, with more free time at home, I started to spend my leisure hours reading. Little did I realize that this would lead to my discovery of the joy of reading.

My mother was prone to giving us instructions on proper behavior before we attended banquets and other social functions. I did not realize the extent of her influence on me until years later.

One day, on my college campus in Canada, I met an old schoolmate from Hong Kong. "I remember you," my schoolmate said. "Your starched white school uniform was never dirty and wrinkled, even at the end of the day. You were always so prim and proper."

Imagine my distress when I thought of myself as a little girl whose white uniform was never wrinkled! I promised myself then that I would never raise my daughters to evoke that image. I believe that I have succeeded in not focusing on raising prim and proper daughters. My daughters, whose clothes look "lived-in" after a day's activities, are more athletic and dynamic than I ever was. However, with a total of four holes in the walls of our house, all from accidents caused by my children, I have occasional doubts about which is the better way to instill proper manners—mine or my mother's.

My parents had the reputation of being kind and generous. Friends of our family were always welcome in our home. When I was in eighth grade, my best friend's mother died of cancer. Her father went to live with his first wife, leaving my friend and her twenty-year-old sister on their own. While the older sister looked for an apartment for them to live in, my mother invited my friend to stay with us. My mother not only preached graciousness and kindness; she also practiced it.

Whether we are aware of it or not, the way we are brought up shapes who we are. The first school for learning about love, values, human relations, habits, and important life skills is our family, whose influence on us is great and lasting. When we raise a family we are also raising the next generation of our society, and we need to keep this crucial role in mind. The welfare of society depends on the success of families. To quote Meyer Francis Nimkoff, "Science has established two facts meaningful for human welfare: first, the foundation of the structure of human personality is laid down in early childhood; and second, the chief engineer in charge of this construction is the family."

Ever since that enlightening conversation ten years ago, my relationship with my mother has improved on many levels. I feel that I am finally getting to know her as a woman. I have come to realize that my childhood feeling of detachment from my mother resulted largely from my own immaturity. With five children, it was difficult for my mother to devote enough attention to each of us individually. When I was growing up I did not understand that, because I was too absorbed in my own world to look at the situation objectively. Today, with three children of my own, I share frustrations similar to those my mother once faced. I believe that for some of us it takes age and experience to appreciate our parents— it took me more than three decades. I urge you to take the time and effort to get to know your parents. They nurtured you from a helpless infant into an independent adult, provided you the comfort of a home with loving kindness, and protected you from harm with absolute resolve; they deserve your love and respect.

During my last visit home, I stayed up one night to hang wallpaper in my parents' basement. My mother stayed up with me. We talked about marriage and motherhood—subjects dear to women's hearts.

"You know, I don't think I'll live long afterwards if your father passes away first," my mother told me. "I would feel lost without him and his protection. He's the smarter half."

That statement gave me a glimpse of the inner workings of my parents' marriage. I had no idea that my mother held my father in such high esteem. But why was I surprised? I never paid much attention to their relationship, but after my own marriage, I could understand theirs better. Had I thought more about this subject earlier in life, I probably would have made different choices. Perhaps my own marriage would have had a different outcome.

My parents have been married for almost fifty years. I always thought my father was the dominant partner, but I have learned otherwise. Twelve years ago my parents went on a trip to Asia, and two years later my father wanted to tour Asia again. But they did not make the second trip, because my mother did not want to go. This was the first time I realized the extent to which my mother influences their decisions. I have since observed that my parents' relationship is more balanced than I originally thought. When they bought new furniture, my mother chose the couch and my father chose the coffee and end tables. My childhood perspective on my parents' marriage was quite different from the reality.

I remember jokingly telling my ex-husband that Chinese people do not kiss, because I never saw my own parents kiss. It is not my parents' nature to demonstrate their affection publicly. Chinese culture is more conservative than American culture, and physical displays of affection are rarely seen—especially in my parents' generation. However, there are good reasons why my parents' marriage has endured life's trials for close to half a century. The secrets of a lasting marriage transcend the boundaries of country and culture. My parents' union gave birth to the loving home of my childhood—for which I am grateful.

My aunt used to quote this Chinese proverb to describe my childhood: "A fresh flower in a warm room." She meant that I grew up in a stable family, sheltered from life's problems. For many years, I assumed that my children would have the kind of stability that I had in childhood. Then came my divorce. Going through the divorce has been the most painful experience in my life thus far. I shed tears of sadness over the breakup of the family, the death of a dream in marriage, the loss of a future based on twenty years of shared history. The fact that I desperately needed the divorce did not lessen the pain. I wish I could have spared my children the trauma of our family's breakup.

My father called me one day in the midst of my divorce. "Come back with your children. You've got our support. You know you can always come home!"

Yes, I knew. Never mind that more than two thousand miles separated me from my original family, or that many years had passed since I left home to lead an independent life. I can always go home to the family I came from. In Chinese families it is not customary to speak of love, and my family is no different. Love is conveyed by deeds. For instance, my father subscribed to *Reader's Digest* because I enjoyed reading. I felt his love for me. Whether love is expressed by small gestures or on a grand scale, the warmth that it radiates is the same. In a family, love is sure, support comes naturally, and geographic distance is no barrier. That is the beauty of family.

A friend once said, "An end also means a new beginning." Like the resurgence of life after a volcanic eruption, our new family unit—my three children and I—emerged out of the ashes of the old one. My children live with me, but they can see their father whenever they want. They tell me that there is not much difference between the times before and after the divorce. Without the background tension of an unhappy marriage, I am more aware of the small pleasures I share with my children, such as listening to a song from a new CD or going to a movie together. I also have more freedom to do things. For instance, I picked the color of our new carpet and redecorated our house without having to justify my decisions to anyone.

In our new family unit, we still have love, laughter, debates, and sibling rivalry. My children are busy with school, friends, and extra-curricular activities just as before. Life goes on. Family life has many crises. However, we humans are survivors, blessed with the ability to endure and to overcome. Crises provide the opportunity for us, as individuals and as families, to exercise that ability. With every major and minor crisis, a family gains strength, builds character, and adds interesting elements to its history. My family has survived the crisis of a divorce. Its structure may have changed, but our family remains intact—such is the strength of family.

When we go out to dinner with my family in Toronto, we usually need a table for a party of twenty-two to twenty-five people. On one occasion during our last visit, I watched my three children making connections with with their cousins, aunts, uncles, and grandparents. It gave me pleasure to share with my children a fundamental experience of Chinese culture—large family gatherings. Since the birth of my first child, I have made yearly visits with my children to Toronto in the hope that they would get acquainted with the family that shaped me. However, with all my good intentions, I neglected one important element—the language barrier that prevents my children and their grandparents from engaging in meaningful conversation. My children did not learn Chinese and my parents have limited English. I hope to compensate for this and provide part of the missing link between my parents and my children by writing this book. One of the treasures of family is grandparents. These are the people who have the freedom to spoil us as well as the accumulated wisdom to teach us. They are the link to our family heritage. Time spent with grandparents makes wonderful memories. If you have grandparents, take advantage of your good fortune. Spend time getting to know them.

Sometimes I wonder if I am a good enough provider and protector for my children. I understand the importance of raising a family. I want to take care of my children to the best of my ability so they will know the protection and security I knew in childhood. I have found out that there is more than one way to take care of a family. In Hong Kong, when my friends were waiting in long lines to get student bus passes, mine and my sisters' were delivered to my father's office, thanks to his connections in the community. I do not have the same kind of connections my father had. My children do not enjoy those special favors, but I have discovered that they are more mature and independent than I was at their age. I never cooked a meal or did the laundry during my childhood. Today, my two daughters sometimes prepare their own meals and they do their own laundry. A couple of weeks ago, my thirteen-year-old daughter sat down with next year's high school freshman class choices and selected the classes that would be of maximum advantage for her college plans. Meanwhile, my nine-year-old son informed me, in no uncertain terms, that I will shop for him no longer. He is going to choose his clothes and hair style himself!

I have concluded that as long as there is love, support, and wisdom, the family will remain strong. The parent's role is to provide guidance, instill values, and nurture confidence in the children. There is no single correct model for the family. We are all unique individuals. We all come from different families. That is precisely why our world is as diverse and interesting as it is.

My dear daughter, family plays a crucial role in our lives. It is the place where we become who we are. Treasure your relationship with your siblings. These are the people who share your past and can become your best friends in the future. Maintain connections with other branches of family, for you share common roots. Seek to understand your parents and establish a good relationship with them. They are the people who provided you love, support, and protection during childhood when you needed them most. Your parents' influence on you is strong and lasting. Realize the value of family, where love and support come naturally. Don't underestimate the strength of family, for it can withstand major life crises. Remember the important role of family when you are raising one of your own. The success of society is directly related to the success of families. Take care of yours and cherish your relationship. That, I promise, will enhance your family life.

Career

事業

The highest reward for man's toil
is not what he gets for it,
but what he becomes by it.
                              —John Ruskin

When I asked my older daughter what she would like to see in my chapter about careers, she replied, "I want to find out exactly how to find a job I really love and make lots and lots of money doing it."

Wouldn't we all like to do that! More than two decades after college, I am still searching for the ideal career—the one I had in my youthful vision—doing something with grand passion and getting great financial rewards for it. As much as I would like to, unfortunately I do not have the wisdom to offer a precise formula for finding the perfect career. My own journey in search of that holy grail is still in progress.

I wonder how many eighteen-year-olds know exactly what they want to be. I certainly did not when

I was eighteen. By the age of twenty-one—the official threshold of adulthood in our society—I still did not have the answer. There was no magic moment; no fairy godmother appeared to transform me and dispel my indecision. After the birthday celebration, I was still my usual immature self, wondering what I wanted to be when I grew up.

College was supposed to be my training ground for a career. However, there was one big problem—I did not know what I wanted to do. When I looked at the possible fields of study, the choices were over-whelming. Alas, my career preparation was hampered by my lack of direction. I started out at college with the intention of studying biochemistry, because chemistry was one of my favorite subjects. That may have been a logical path to follow, but it was the wrong choice for me. How could I possibly major in biochemistry when all those incredibly long biological terms intimidated me? I said to myself, "Obviously, I could use some help from my fairy godmother."

Eventually, I transferred to business school and graduated with an accounting degree—but I never pursued a career in accounting. I became a wife and mother instead. Today, I work as a Chinese interpreter.

You are in good company, I assure you, if you are wrestling with the question "What do I want to be?" Many who have gone before you did not know either. In the years that have passed since my college days, I have grown older and a little wiser. I have learned a few things about searching for direction in life.

As a starting point, make a list in three columns of your interests, your skills, and your strengths. It will help you to focus on choices. Comparing your interests and skills is a logical second step. With a mix-and-match list in hand, you are prepared to unleash your creative thinking and discover career possibilities. Remember, we go as far as we allow ourselves to go. We grow as long as we permit ourselves to expand our limits. Gender has no bearing on intellectual ability. Think big. Think equal. Think creatively. Next, reduce the number of items on the list. The process of elimination—paring the list down to the final choices—will do wonders for your sanity. The final list can be used as a map to guide you toward what you want to be.

I often find myself telling my children, "Even if you don't know exactly what you want, make sure you are doing *something.*"

My greatest concern is that my children might end up doing nothing. I have seen many people who hold promise which remains just that—years later—because they do nothing with their potential. I have used the analogy of a car trip to get my point across to my children.

"Imagine you're going on vacation to a place where you've never been before. Sure, you can find it on the map, but if you are ever going to arrive at your destination, you have to start driving," I said.

"We're not driving!" my daughters said, sensing my impending monologue.

"Of course not, but that's beside the point," I continued. "It helps if there's a map, so that you can see how to drive in the general direction of your destination. The map, in this case, is the list of your possible career choices, your interests, your dreams. You start driving—*doing something* about the list—by taking related classes."

I left out the fact that sometimes, while searching for our way, we may get lost and need to take some detours. Even then, the chances of figuring out how to get where we want to go are infinitely better if we keep on looking.

I took a detour from my career path—I got married and became a mother. The focus of my life shifted to my family. For many years I was a full-time mother; I consider that the most important work I have done. When my twenty-year marriage ended, I lacked the skills and experience to return to the profession for which I was trained. My degree in accounting meant very little without up-to-date computer skills and work experience. As is often exhibited in life, when one door closes, another door opens. Almost by accident, I discovered my dormant marketable skill—languages. Someone approached me about being a Chinese interpreter. The long and winding road of life has a way of surprising us.

If I were given a chance to travel back in time, I would change the way I dealt with my career. Throughout those years as a full-time mother, I logged countless volunteer hours. However, the sad truth is that the volunteer experience in my résumé does not count as legitimate work experience. As important as motherhood is to me, I now feel that I should not have forsaken my career for it. I do not regret staying home to raise my children, but wish that I had not neglected to update my job skills. My advice to all young women is: Maintain your profession. A career is the means for achieving financial independence. Life does not always turn out as planned. We need to equip ourselves with marketable skills; our independence depends on it.

One day my older daughter, then fifteen going on sixteen, decided to publish a "ska 'zine"—a small magazine about ska music, which she loves. With only her passion and absolutely no experience, she christened her 'zine *SKAZAAM!* She went to concerts and interviewed the bands, wrote most of the articles, reviewed CDs, and taught herself the nuts and bolts of producing a 'zine. To my amazement, she decided on *free* distribution. In order to finance her project she saved her lunch money, monetary gifts from family, and her clothing allowance. Meanwhile, she kept up with her school work and all her other activities. Four months later, the first issue of *SKAZAAM!* was launched, to rave reviews from the ska community. It was truly a labor of love. After the first issue, she was invited to write occasional music review columns for the *Oregonian,* a major metropolitan newspaper. By following her heart, my daughter not only fulfilled her dream of producing a 'zine, but she also learned about conducting interviews, writing reviews and articles, editing, publishing, and selling advertising space. Throughout this experience her gain was plentiful and her loss was—sleep! I have seen passion at work. It is truly a power to be reckoned with. I bow to its power.

I have learned a great lesson from my daughter by observing her publishing project. This teenager decided to deny herself clothes and spending money in pursuit of a dream. She demonstrated inestimable drive and commitment. She taught me that when we have a burning desire to do something but lack the skills, we should follow our heart. The necessary skills can be learned, if we are determined. Our burning desire is our passion, the inner fire from our heart, the driving force, our best ally for making things happen—all things.

Whenever the subject of work and career came up during my childhood, one of my dad's favorite sayings was: "Among the seventy-two occupations, there is a *Jong Yuen* in every occupation." I know this maxim has to be an ancient one; it comes from a time when there were only seventy-two occupations in China! *Jong Yuen* was a title of highest honor given to the top scholar in a series of national examinations held when China was still under the emperors' rule. This series of examinations was held at regular intervals. For citizens with no connection to positions of power or wealth in the kingdom, it was a popular route to recognition through academic achievement. Typically, the person who acquired this title would be invited to take a position at court. The *Jong Yuen* system was designed so that the most talented men of obscure birth could be identified and be of service to the government. At the same time, it allowed them to advance their social standing. Seventy-two occupations or not, my father's message was "Whatever your chosen field, strive to be the best." There is a place for the outstanding and the successful in every occupation.

What constitutes career success? Success is a relative term that means different things to different people. I believe that it usually implies achieving goals. My youngest sister, a self-described ambitious career woman, told me that she has always set short- and long-term career goals. About every two to three years, she checks to see if her career is on course, and takes the necessary actions to redirect herself, to meet her objectives. This kind of drive, commitment, and discipline almost always ensures success. My sister has done well for herself in the corporate world at a relatively young age. She has ambitious goals, obvious commitment to her objectives, and a go-getter's persistence in keeping her career on course—she also works long, hard hours.

"You can't just stop what you're doing, and go home after an eight-hour day. You have to give whatever it takes to do a first-rate job," my sister once told me. She strives to do her best in pursuing her career, and her efforts are well rewarded financially.

A career is a person's lifework. Like a garden that needs to be cultivated, a career needs to be nurtured.

A gardener cannot cultivate a beautiful garden without watering the plants and flowers daily, pulling weeds, trimming the bushes, and mowing the lawn. Pursuing a career is not much different. It takes showing up for work regularly, learning new skills, polishing those skills, and performing tasks well. Nurturing career goals takes time and patience, but realizing those long-sought goals can be a joy as satisfying as a mother's seeing her baby for the first time.

Last year, my son brought a project home from school. It was a poster he had drawn, with a caption about himself. Two phrases caught my eye: "who dreams of being a millionaire" and "who plans to be a baseball player."

"You want to be a baseball player, huh?" I asked my son.

"I love baseball, Mom," he replied.

"So, you want to be a millionaire?" I asked. It was news to me.

"Yes, everybody wants to be a millionaire! So I can do what I want," he responded.

At the tender age of nine, my son was after the same things in life as the rest of us. He wants a career that he loves, and lots of money. I should not be surprised; it's natural to want to do something enjoyable. After all, we spend many hours of the day doing our work. Making money is important, of course, for we work to make a living—it's a necessity of life. Being a millionaire may not be everybody's goal, but most people want to make enough money to be financially self-sufficient. While money cannot buy happiness, it does give us the freedom to enjoy many things in life.

My older daughter once told me she was worried about making a wrong career choice. I understood that concern, because I was once in the same place. Wouldn't it be lovely if we could make perfect career choices from the beginning, and then cruise through the rest of our lives? Fortunately, life is more interesting than that. But unfortunately, life is not that easy. Those of us who do not make perfect career moves right away may find ourselves contemplating changes later on. Doing something different can be good—if you play your cards right. If you are uncertain about your career choice, remind yourself that you can make modifications in the future.

Since returning to the work force, I have been involved in several different business ventures. I did not even realize how I operate until a friend brought it to my attention.

"You will plunge in. I know you," my friend said, in reference to my contemplating this book project.

And I did!

I suppose I do plunge into new endeavors, but before I begin a project I try to calculate the risks. Keeping the risk factor at a moderate level is important to me because I like to avoid excess in anything. As soon as I become involved in a new enterprise, I have a strong desire to be proficient at it—I take the plunge, learning and performing the requisite tasks as well as I can.

Looking at my past and present business ventures, regardless of their success, I find that I always learn something from them. I am reminded of the saying "Nothing ventured, nothing gained!" There will be times when you face decisions about undertaking new enterprises. If it feels right after you weigh all the factors, I suggest that you go ahead—plunge in! Follow your heart, and work with your heart.

My dear daughter, your career is an important part of your life's journey. Choose your work with care. Keep exploring new career paths if you are uncertain. Reach for the stars. Strive to be the best at whatever you do. Never forsake your career for the other parts of your life, because it is the means to independence. Do something that gives you joy and good financial rewards. Select something that gives your life meaning. Make career changes when you deem them appropriate. Nurture your career and enjoy your work. That, I promise, will contribute to your happiness.

愛與相處之道

Love
and
Relationships

*We never live so intensely as when
we love strongly.
We never realize ourselves so vividly as when
we are in the full glow of love for others.*
—Walter Rauschenbush

If I had to name the relative, outside my immediate family, to whom I feel closest, I would name my aunt. My mother's youngest sister has been a close member of my family since my infancy. Only ten years my senior, my aunt is more like a big sister to me. I enjoyed being her favorite niece during my childhood, and that privilege came in handy during her courtship. My aunt and her boyfriend frequently included me on fun outings such as going to the beach or visiting famous attractions in Hong Kong. I was what the Chinese call an "electric light bulb," a special term used in the context of dating: the light bulb's bright wattage disturbs dimly lit romantic moments. Did I give a hoot what I was called? Not in the least! Being known as a light bulb was a small price to pay for the delightful excursions. My aunt did not seem to regard me as an intruder. She was having fun, as well. But underneath her gaiety lay a miserable childhood and an unyielding spirit.

My aunt was only nine years old when her mother died of cancer. By then, both her siblings—my mother and my uncle—had already established their own families. Two years later her father remarried. His new wife disliked my young aunt with a passion. She was banished from her room to sleep on the bunk bed in the hallway. It was then that my aunt came to our home on weekends and holidays to evade her step-mother's hostility. My aunt knew education was her ticket to escape from the misery of her home. When her father suffered a stroke and was paralyzed, her stepmother started to insinuate that my aunt should drop out of school and go to work in the factory, at the tender age of fifteen. Aware that her only defense was her excellent academic standing, my aunt studied harder than ever. With the support of her siblings, she won her fight to finish secondary school.

"I wasn't going to work in a factory like my cousin Lin," I recall my aunt saying years later. "I'm making something of myself. I love myself even though Mum doesn't love me!"

In that statement I heard the voice of a deter-mined human spirit defying her circumstances because she loved herself. She knew her worth regardless of what her stepmother told her. Self-love is vital to self-esteem. It empowers our hearts and souls. My aunt's love for herself impelled her to fight for her future. She went on to nursing school and became a registered nurse. Today, she has two grown sons and lives in Toronto with her husband. My aunt and I remain close in our hearts, if not in geographical location.

When I think of my aunt's difficult childhood, her statement proclaiming her strength in the face of adversity inevitably comes to mind. The importance of self-love lies in what it can do for the human spirit. The ability to love oneself is fundamental to a person's well-being. Our hearts and souls need love the way our bodies require food and water. Much as a mother's love is essential to her baby's emotional security, self-love is vital to a mature person's ability to love others.

What is love, really? To me it's a warm feeling indispensable to the human soul. I remember a sense of security from knowing my parents' love for me, and a sense of excitement when I was romantically in love. I think of the happiness I feel when I see my beloved children happy. No matter how I analyze it, I know one thing: we humans need that loving feeling.

When I was a child, love from my family seemed sufficient. Then, at age fourteen, I discovered romantic love. It opened up a whole new range of emotions. A boy in my class began to pay attention to me. He started coming to play soccer with the children in my neighborhood. One day, he stopped by our apartment to say hello, and I talked to him for a few minutes at the door.

"Invite your friend to come in next time," my mother told me as I walked back in. "It's impolite to leave someone standing at your door."

After that day, he became a frequent visitor in my home. We would talk on the phone for two to three hours at a stretch, almost every day. That caused great pain to my sisters because we had only one phone line. The two of us also often went to the movies, a popular form of entertainment in Hong Kong. My parents were liberal in comparison with many of my friends' families. They did not object to my going out with a boy as long as they approved of where we were going. My father, who was involved in the movie industry, actually got the tickets for us so he knew exactly where we were. I felt that I was "in love" for the first time in my life. However, teenage romance in Hong Kong in those days was completely different from what it is in America today.

It was a long time before we started holding hands. And when we did, it was not on busy streets. We feared running into someone we knew. My boyfriend and I did not speak to each other at school. We communicated with each other by handwritten notes. I enlisted my best friend as a messenger to deliver my notes. But secrets were hard to keep. One day, a classmate caught my best friend in the act of tucking my note into my boyfriend's desk drawer. After that, we were the objects of constant teasing.

Whenever one of us was called on to answer a question, the whole class would turn to the other one, exclaiming "Woo!" Defiant creatures that we were, we never acknowledged our romance publicly.

Falling in love made my whole existence wondrous. All my senses were heightened. I was more aware of the beauty of the things I saw, the magnificence of the music I heard, the lusciousness of the food I tasted, the sweetness of the fragrances I smelled. Many people experience romantic love during adolescence when they begin dating.

A friend once asked my opinions on dating. My answer was that I felt everybody should go out with more than just one person. Dating can be especially valuable for a girl with no brothers, like me. When I got a chance to relate to my male peers up close and in person, I had a better understanding of members of the opposite sex and their different personalities.

What did I learn from dating? Sadly, not enough. I was just in it for a good time. I did not gain much insight about choosing a suitable mate. It never occurred to me to think of dating as a learning opportunity, and I eventually got myself into a marriage that was wrong for both partners. Ask yourself questions. "What do I like and dislike about this person?" "Is this the person I want to spend my life with?"

My adolescent dating experience was far different from that of my children's generation in the United States today. Growing up in the Chinese culture, in a more innocent time, I understood that premarital sex was forbidden. In today's American culture, sexual experience often precedes real love between two people. There is a difference between engaging in sex and making love. Making love is a beautiful way to express emotional love, but having sex without feeling love is no more than a physical act. I find it disturbing that people engage in sex so freely nowadays. The consequences of intercourse can go far beyond the scope of the relationship. Pregnancy is one example. The future of a new human being is at stake. As a mother of three children, I can guarantee that having a child will change a person's life forever. I urge you to practice abstinence until you are ready to have an exclusive relationship.

I understand that abstinence is not popular in current American culture. I realize that by promoting this practice I am risking being considered out of step with modern times. Abstinence is, however, the best insurance against the negative consequences of unsafe sex. Some people will say, "That's not going to happen to me." The truth is that it can happen to anyone who is not careful. It is well documented that people suffer from the negative consequences of unsafe sex every day. Some of them can even be deadly. HIV is one example. I believe that prevention is the best cure.

The decision to remain sexually abstinent requires self-discipline—a brain function. However, you have to make the commitment before you find yourself in "the heat of the moment." There are benefits from getting to know your partner well before having sex. Sexual expression of love is divine. I urge you to reserve the joy of loving through your body for your true love.

I define truly loving someone as loving passionately and exclusively. One must embrace life to truly live. One must love unreservedly to truly love. No doubt there is a risk in so doing—we become vulnerable, open to the possibility of being hurt by our partners. But is there any other way to experience the full measure of love? I think not. In my opinion, the only avenue to true love is to embrace love passionately without holding back.

Loving exclusively is necessary when two people are serious about each other. A romantic love relationship is meant for only two individuals. There is no room for anyone else. If one or both partners have more than one love interest, jealousy and distrust are likely to result and that shakes the relationship to its core. When we give love, it is precious because we are giving ourselves. Our love deserves to be received with respect. We don't need partners who are careless with our emotions. Love is a gift, not a game.

Long ago, before I was married, at a college social I met a man who was separated from his wife. We felt a magical connection, like two electric wires connecting to form a complete electric current. I felt as if he knew my soul. We saw each other every day. I was also impressed by his close relationship with his sister, whom he talked to daily. Three months into the courtship, I found out that the "sister" who was calling him constantly was actually his estranged wife.

"I know what kind of person you are," he explained. "You wouldn't go out with me if I told you I just moved out on my wife. She just won't leave me alone."

For four long days, I struggled with the question of whether or not to go on seeing him. I decided that I could not allow myself to be part of anyone's unfinished marriage. At the same time, my internal debate went on. *He said that his marriage was coming to an end anyway. But his explanation was a convenient excuse. He was not truthful about his wife. He said that he loved me one hundred percent. But who was he kidding? He was still seeing his wife. A hundred divided by more than one is not a hundred.* Finally, I had my answer: I shouldn't and couldn't. He moved back to his home. His marriage was not over after all.

Was I surprised? Not exactly. There are only two likely outcomes in a relationship with a married man. The first and not very likely scenario is that the married man will leave his wife and family. But if a man is capable of leaving his wife for another woman, he is equally capable of leaving the other woman for yet another. The second and more probable scenario is that the relationship will end after the first flush of passion. The other woman is left with nothing but the realization that he did not love her enough to leave his wife. In either case, it is a losing proposition.

I recently attended a friend's wedding in a magnificent church. My friend—radiant in her bridal gown—and the groom gazed into each other's loving eyes and exchanged their wedding vows. It was a solemn moment of perfect beauty, quiet joy, and moving tears. Watching my newlywed friends, I knew intuitively that they were right for each other. I was reminded of these words of H. Jackson Brown, Jr.: "Marry the right person. This one decision will determine ninety percent of your happiness or misery."

How does one know who is the right person to marry? There is no easy answer to this question. I wish there were a formula that specified the makeup of a right mate. But we humans are too complicated to compute. A friend told me that she wrote down what she wanted in a life partner. She knew that she had found the right person when she met a man who matched many of the points on her list. I like the idea of making a list. The process of organizing thoughts prior to writing helps to clarify them, and identify what kind of person you want.

When I was growing up, I never thought about qualities that would make a person suitable for me. My courtship with my husband was a long-distance affair—there were more than fifteen hundred miles between us—and we did not get to know each other well. During our frequent but short visits together, we had the pleasure of seeing each other at our best. After we were married, I realized that my husband and I had completely different values in regard to just about every aspect of life. We were so different that a friend once remarked that we must be from two different planets. We rarely agreed, even on the fundamentals. Although it is not necessary for marriage partners to be alike, I believe that there needs to be some common ground. Unfortunately, my husband and I could not find enough common ground; our marriage was unsuitable to a disastrous extent.

Cultivating that marriage was one of the most demanding challenges of my life. When a friend asked me why we stayed together so long, I answered, "I was raised that way." My mother taught me early that marriage is forever—a belief that was ingrained in me. Attempting to honor my marriage vows was much like trying to rescue a sinking ship. I fought a long, hard battle to save my marriage, and I lost. I became the only member of my family to divorce—a distinction I did not wish to hold. Sometimes, even with the best of intentions, marriage is not forever. Keeping a marriage vow requires cooperation by both partners. I have no regrets about my marriage, from which came three wonderful children, or about my divorce, through which two unhappy souls broke free. I take comfort in knowing that I did the best I could.

I am not an expert on love and relationships, but I have gained some insights from the misery of my failed marriage. One of the important attributes to look for in a life partner is shared values. It is not real-istic to expect a partner to share all of your values, but it is a good idea to choose a person who shares and respects some and preferably most of the ideas that are important to you. To quote Antoine de Saint-Exupéry, "Love does not consist in gazing at each other, but in looking outward together in the same direction."

I grew up with strong family values. Taking care of my family was my top priority next to marriage. I thought parenthood would be a joint venture. I did not expect to find myself alone with my children on weekends and holidays while my husband pursued his recreational activities. Thus, our different family values created a rift between us. If you think having a family is part of your future, choose someone who is family oriented. Raising a family is very important business.

As part of my attempt to save my marriage, I consulted a few of my relatives and friends on the secrets of a lasting relationship.

"We are buddies! He is my best friend," my youngest sister told me.

No matter how much you are in love with your partner, passion and infatuation wear off over time. Besides being in love, you also need to like your partner. It's natural to like someone whose disposition and character draw your friendship and respect. Indeed, friendship is an important part of a love relationship. Eventually, it is friendship that creates the bond of love between two people.

There are other important considerations in choosing a life partner: intelligence, honesty, kindness, responsibility, dependability, a good sense of

humor, a good work ethic, and the ability to make and
honor commitments. Obviously, everybody has a
different set of priorities. Humans are diverse creatures—not all after the same type of individual, thank
goodness. The more we know what we want, the better
are our chances of identifying the right mate. I recall
that when my father taught me to play Chinese chess,
he said, "Don't move hastily. Think and wait for the
right move. Give it your best shot. You play to win!" By
the same token, if your goal is to have a successful relationship, it pays to wait for the right person.

A friend once said, "There is someone for
everyone, and there is a right one for everyone. Do
you want the someone or the right one?"

The importance of "the right person" to a good
relationship is equal to the importance of the right
materials to a good product. Love between partners
who are right for each other has a much better chance
of developing into a fulfilling relationship.

My early vision of romantic love was influenced
by the romance fiction with happily-ever-after
endings that I read during my naive teenage years. I
thought love struck, and lovers lived happily ever
after. True, falling in love can happen suddenly, since
the initial attraction of two people is often physical.
But living happily ever after is possible only if two
people in love actively work on their relationship.

Fulfilling relationships between love partners do
not happen automatically. They require nurturing to
flourish. Falling in love is only the initial phase of a love

relationship. It is not a permanent condition, since one can also fall out of love. Imagine falling in love as flower seeds sown in a garden. Beautiful, full blossoms come from regular attention—proper watering and feeding. A true union of bodies and souls comes from careful attention to ensure that the relationship will bloom.

When my husband and I bought our house, there were different features each of us did not like about it. I grew up in Hong Kong and later lived in Toronto, Canada. Both are among the most cosmopolitan cities in the world. I am a city girl at heart. I like my house to be close to the city, but my husband liked to live in the country. This house was the only one we could find that was not too far from the city and yet close enough to the country to have wooded acreage. But, I disliked the orange countertops, the carpeted kitchen, and the peeling exterior paint. We agreed that a remodeling project was in order.

He got the setting he liked. I got a house with potential, and a promise to remodel it.

One of the arts of reaching agreement is compromise, which is necessary for a couple to live in harmony. Differences of opinion are certain in relationships. Occasional fights are unavoidable, but you cannot allow disagreements to take a prominent role because the relationship will eventually suffer from battle fatigue. Through mutual concessions, we do not get exactly what we want, but we spare ourselves needless conflict. We are giving up something for the greater good—the welfare of the relationship.

Shortly after we moved into our house, I heard my husband tell the piano tuner, "My wife doesn't like this wallpaper. We're going to change it soon."

A month later, I was getting impatient for that change. Finally, I talked to my husband.

"Yes, soon. It hasn't been long," he responded.

Apparently, my definition of "soon" was very different from his. I was thinking in terms of days, while he was thinking months. It never occurred to me that we needed to elaborate. I just assumed that everybody had the same timetable. Misunderstanding often is based on false assumptions and a lack of communication. In order to have a clear under- standing of anyone, you need to talk.

Good communication is essential in love rela- tionships. Nobody reads minds, not even life partners. After the initial phase of the euphoria of being in love, a marriage needs to have the substance to survive the mundane monotony of washing the clothes, cleaning the bathroom, taking out the trash, and other daily tasks, which can be trying at times. Thank goodness for language. We need to talk about and share each other's feelings and concerns, so that we can direct actions where they are needed.

A forgiving heart is necessary in a marriage. I learned long ago that there is little advantage in letting anger simmer. People make mistakes. It is just part of being human. Harboring negative emotions in response to your partner's mistakes is harmful to the health of the relationship as well as the human body. Do yourself a favor—spare your body from prolonged stress. You need to make up with your mate sooner or later if you are to stay together. Get over the negative emotion as quickly as possible. Take this familiar advice: Never go to bed angry. Forgive your partner but beware of the mistakes that challenge your fundamental values. Under *no* circumstances should we compromise the values that we hold dear.

In a long-term love relationship such as marriage, unless love is rekindled on a regular basis it will die of inattention. When I was learning to use the woodstove in my house, at first I did not understand why I could not get the fire going. I discovered that it was because I did not put the fuel in when it was needed. Marriage is like the fire in the woodstove— without adequate fuel, it will extinguish itself. The fuel is the things we do to rekindle the romance, such as regular dinner and movie dates together.

During a period in my marriage when my husband and I had regular Friday evening dates, I relished the pleasure of going out as a couple, taking a recess from motherhood, and leaving my preschoolers with a babysitter for a few hours. Our relationship was better, largely due to our efforts. However, rekindling the romance needs to be an ongoing effort; it works best as a preventive measure, not as a solution for problems. To quote Mignon McLaughlin, "A successful marriage requires falling in love many times, always with the same person."

As important as marriage is, I believe that it is equally important to retain your individual identity. A marriage is meant to enrich life. One must not lose oneself because of it. An ideal marriage is one where both partners love and nurture each other, so that both become better individuals as well as a better couple. A successful marriage has a great many rewards. It embodies the happiness we seek in life. It adds strength to combat adversity. A happy marriage is built with diligent work. It requires careful attention, to the selection of a suitable mate and to the constant nurturing of the relationship. But, marriage is worth the effort—for a happy union of two souls is one of life's greatest joys.

Love comes in many different forms, such as the love between parents, grandparents, and a child; the love among siblings; and the love among friends. No matter what kind of love, it nurtures us with its warm glow. A love relationship of any kind needs attention to flourish. I wish to remind you that other love relationships are important parts of our lives as well. Romantic love should not be the only love that we seek and cherish. Our mates should not be expected to provide for all our emotional needs. It is too much to ask from one individual. Like a healthy diet, we need to have daily supplies from different nutritional groups. To have healthy emotions, we need to have love from different sources regularly. More importantly, we must reciprocate the love given by those who are dear to us. The joy of loving comes from giving as well as receiving.

My dear daughter, I have devoted the main part of this essay to romantic love, because you are likely to fall in love at this time of your life. Love nourishes our bodies and souls. It all begins with loving yourself. When you do fall in love, love passionately and exclusively with your partner. Practice abstinence until you meet your true love. Select your mate carefully. This is an important decision—for a good relationship you need the right candidate. Take time to choose before making a commitment. Nurture your love relationships diligently. Your goal is to achieve a successful union. Cherish other kinds of relationships for they, too, nourish your emotional health. That, I promise, will enhance your life.

Parenthood

父
母
心

Making the decision to have a child—
it's momentous.
It is to decide forever to have your heart walking
outside your body.
—Elizabeth Stone

B ecoming a parent is one of life's defining
moments. It changes a person forever. No books I
had read prepared me for the arrival of motherhood.
One spring day in 1982 when the tulips were in full
bloom, after I had been in labor for a day and a half,
my doctor asked for my consent to a cesarean section.
Gone was my vanity—humbled by labor pain, I was
more than ready for the surgery whether it left scars
or not. Much like a distance runner in her last lap, I
was relieved that I had finally come to the end of the
course, eager to touch the finish line—my baby.

My final lap, however, was not without incident.
After the local anesthesia was administered, I found

myself having difficulty breathing. Apparently the anesthetic was stronger than anticipated, and it was spreading to my upper body. I was seized with terror that death was near. My recurring thoughts were: *I must live! My child, a brand new human being who is about to enter this world, depends on me!* Determined to overcome every obstacle, I channeled all my energy into keeping my eyes wide open, for fear that I would never wake up again once I surrendered to drowsiness. All through the surgery, with the oxygen mask firmly placed on my face, I stared wide-eyed at the anesthesiologist above me with all the strength that I could muster. Who cared what a strange sight that was. There was only one thought in my mind: *Stay awake.*

"Wah, wah!" My baby's cry shook me loose from my single-minded focus.

Someone placed a bundle beside me. I turned to meet my baby face to face for the first time. Tears of joy streamed down my face. My heart was overflowing with gratitude for this tremendous gift—my daughter—a breathing miracle that was beyond my comprehension. I knew at that instant my life would never be the same again.

The passage into motherhood was not only the jubilant moment of welcome that I had anticipated. It was full of mixed emotions: *relief,* for the healthy, normal baby; *joy,* for the new arrival to the family; *awe,* for the mystery and might of human creation; *anxiety,* over my new role of parenthood. As I watched my infant daughter lying in my arms, I was acutely aware of my crucial role in her life. My baby was totally dependent on me for her protection and survival. My influence on her as a human being would be immeasurable. How ill-prepared I was for such an enormous task! No school that I attended taught me the arts and science of motherhood. Yes, I had read many books on the subject of parenting, but how much did I really know? I suddenly felt inadequate to take on the role of parent. Not a particularly religious person, I nevertheless said many prayers—for wisdom and guidance.

True to my goal-oriented self, I approached motherhood by formulating the objectives I wanted to achieve as a parent. My long-term goal was to raise my daughter to be a happy, independent, intelligent indi-vidual—a good human being with compassion and respect for others, and a productive citizen who makes positive contributions to society. Meanwhile, I would need to educate myself if I were to have any hope of achieving that goal. Since I did not have family close by and had recently moved to San Francisco, books were my primary source of educa-tion on parenthood. I followed the baby books faith-fully. My short-term goal was to ensure that my baby would have optimal care.

A few weeks after my daughter was born, a friend asked me to go out to lunch with her.

"I'd love to go but I don't have a babysitter," I told my friend.

"Bring your baby with you," my friend suggested.

"Yes, but I still need to feed her! My baby eats every two hours. I'm afraid we won't be home in time for that. There's not enough time between feedings to do anything," I said.

"Don't you use bottles to supplement? Bring your bottles and milk with you, first time mother!" My friend seemed amused.

The thought of packing bottles had not even crossed my mind! I did not recall reading anything about carrying baby bottles in my child-care books— so much for my technical approach to parenting know-how. I have learned that while it is helpful to read advice about the fundamentals of parenting, common sense still applies, as always.

Parenting is an art in and of itself. Most of us receive little if any education prior to becoming parents. Yet parenting is a huge responsibility. I cannot think of anyone who has more influence on another human being than his or her parents. I urge you to take parenthood very seriously. Nurturing the next generation of our species is the most important job in life. I hope you will make a commitment to being a good parent by continually educating, evaluating, and bettering yourself. This is your contribution to humanity.

As a mother of three children—two daughters and one son—I have heard comments about how girls are easier to raise than boys. In my experience, every child is different. My three children have their own unique traits and different temperaments. My daughters are just as capable in a physical fight as my son. I am not certain that one gender is really easier than the other. My own siblings and I are close in age, but I chose to have my children three to four years apart because I thought that sibling rivalry among them would be less frequent and severe. I was partially right about that. Sibling rivalry was less frequent, but the degree of severity was the same. Children are still children. No matter which part of the world they come from, children's behaviors are universal. Love, guidance, and discipline are needed in parenting everywhere.

Like many parents, I reflected on my own upbringing for self-counsel on parenting. In Hong Kong, spanking was the most commonly used parental disciplinary method. My family and all my childhood friends' families had spanking sticks at home. We children, raised in the Chinese culture that honors elders, were an obedient bunch. Submitting to our parents' discipline without question was commonly accepted, justified or not. Hong Kong is a densely populated city with a small land area so living quarters are close together. Through open windows, we often heard our neighbors disciplining their children.

"Do you hear that? If you misbehave, I'll send you over there for spanking too," my mother would sometimes threaten us on such occasions.

As a child, I was convinced that there was a conspiracy among parents to keep children in line by disciplining them publicly. I often wondered if there were better ways to handle children's mischief.

When it came time for my decisions about methods of discipline, I did not want to blindly follow the patterns of my childhood. I believe that discipline is necessary in parenting. Children need to have boundaries, and there should be consequences when they cross those boundaries. Thanks to advice I gathered from books and magazines, I adopted a moderate approach to discipline. Instead of displays of absolute parental authority, threats, and spanking, I opted for problem-solving to allow my children their voice during conflicts, positive rewards to promote good feelings about desirable behaviors, and consequences other than spanking. I am drawn to gentle disciplinary methods—however, always staying true to my resolve to use this positive approach has not been easy.

After work one day, I was preparing dinner in my newly remodeled kitchen when suddenly I noticed the gleam of metal on the family room wall across the kitchen island. On closer inspection, I found a big dent on the corner of the wall; some drywall was missing and the metal flashing strip was exposed. I also noticed that my children were conveniently absent from the family room. Instinctively, I summoned them.

"What happened?" I asked, although I had a fairly good idea already.

Silence.

"Who did this? Tell me what happened," I commanded.

"He was chasing me," my second daughter said, pointing to my son. "I ran and slipped on the edge of the carpet and bumped into the wall with my knee. Sorry!"

"Are you hurt?" I asked my daughter.

"No, just bruised." My daughter showed me a huge bruise on her knee.

"How many times have I told you not to chase each other on this slippery wood floor? Don't you know better? You are in big trouble with me. I'll have to punish you both."

My son spoke up: "Why are you yelling at us? It was just an accident!"

Of course it was an accident—I knew that. I was angry at my children for running in spite of house rules and damaging my beautiful new kitchen. Never mind the positive disciplinary approach. I was not interested in problem-solving that would allow my children to brainstorm a remedy. I knew what they deserved! Ruling out spanking, which I detest, I resorted to threats and using my parental power to make my point. Emotion overshadowed theory. I had become reactive instead of objective.

Eager as I was to adopt new parenting techniques, and despite my good intentions to stay true to them, over the years I have breached my own guidelines more frequently than I meant to. I have come to realize that we parents are just normal mortals with our share of imperfections. All we can do, after undesirable reactions to our children's behavior have blown over, is try to do better next time. As long as we are consistently making genuine attempts to be good parents, we need not judge ourselves too harshly.

Having children has taught me new aspects of life's pleasures. My first daughter did not crawl before she took her first step. She scooted around well into her second year. I checked all my reference materials but I could not find scooting mentioned as the pre-walking stage. Despite the pediatrician's reassurance, I was worried that my daughter would never learn to walk. A vision of myself, a petite mother, carrying an overage, oversized daughter began to emerge in my mind. Then, one day into her eighteenth month, my daughter took her first step. I was jumping and clapping in elation. The jubilant celebration over the first step of her baby is a joy to which only a parent can relate. Over the years, my children's milestones, triumphs, and achievements have become part of my life's pleasure. The joy of parenthood comes in small doses.

Since I have become a mother, my priorities have changed from self-focused to child-focused. My children's welfare is foremost in my mind. Their needs come before my own. I remember when I took my children out for pizza one day. When we were down to the last three slices, I realized that I had not ordered enough. Looking into my children's hungry eyes, I told them that I did not want any more, although in fact I was still hungry. This behavior was a far departure from my usual conduct before motherhood. In my self-absorbed youth, I would certainly have taken my fair share of the family meal. Motherhood has transformed me.

Raising children is like going through childhood all over again, only from a different perspective. As parents, we have the privilege of observing human maturation first-hand; we learn and grow throughout the process. Through nurturing our children, as we instinctively recognize their needs and strive to meet them, we become more considerate to others. By setting a good example, trying as that may be at times, we teach our children to be responsible and caring. That is the beauty of parenthood.

Once when I was a college freshman, I had a conversation with a friend about the future of Hong Kong, which was still a British colony then but slated for return to China one day. My friend wanted to know if I, being a native, was worried about Hong Kong's fate under communist China.

"No, I don't have any family there anymore. It doesn't really matter to me what is going to happen," I said.

More than twenty years later, it does matter to me. When Hong Kong was returned to Chinese rule in 1997, I paid close attention to the reports and prayed for the future of the people in my birthplace. I wanted peace and stability for that region and the world around us. Before I had children, my concerns about the world were largely limited to my home, my daily living, and my immediate community. I paid little attention to anything that did not affect me directly. Today, as a mother, I find that my world has expanded far beyond my immediate surroundings. I care about the welfare of not only the land where I live and its people, but also the world at large. I want to do my part. Whether in my modest material contributions or my volunteer hours, every little bit helps to make this world a safer and better place for my children and our descendants to inhabit.

One day not long ago, my second daughter and I stayed up all night to talk. Under the warm glow of a Tiffany lamp, snuggling among sofa pillows, we discussed our values, our views of the world, and many other subjects. My daughter, who seldom shows much interest in long conversations with me, was more animated than usual. She was very receptive to what I had to say. I felt a real connection to her. When we bid each other good night at dawn, I had so enjoyed the night that I did not want it to end—some of the finest moments ever between my daughter and me, alone together. What was the key to such a successful connection?

Through the years, I have talked with my children about values that are important to me. I believe that, as a parent, I have a responsibility to instill values in my children. However, sustaining their interest in such subjects has not been easy. It was not uncommon for my eager children, in their polite moods, to show impatient faces that implored me to stop talking. They were tuning me out. I was boring them to death with my near-monologue. Successful communication occurs only if children are part of the discussion, with equal participation, expressing their views.

Most parents with teenagers can probably identify with my need to deal with my children's "smart mouths" from time to time. I don't recall ever behaving that way as a child. This is not to say that I never wanted to answer back to my parents. I simply did that in silence. We had our share of disagreements. However, after I made my views known, if my parents still insisted on exerting their parental authority, I understood that it would be fruitless to argue with them. I certainly would not speak disrespectfully to them. That would be impolite! In the Chinese culture, respect for one's elders and being polite are honored virtues. I was the recipient of my elementary school's "Politeness Award." I believe that I was chosen for my perfect bows.

My children and I live in American society, a culture that celebrates freedom of speech and everything else—and I would not want to change that—but I must admit that I do not particularly like hearing my children answer back to me disrespectfully. To borrow an expression from my children, "It sucks!" This is one of the trials of parenthood.

I remember that in Hong Kong my mother went to the open market every day. Most of the ladies in the neighborhood, outfitted with shopping baskets on their arms, shopped at the same time as if by daily appointment. My mother would spend a couple of hours in the market, chatting with her friends and shopping for fresh seafood, meat, and produce. I now realize that these daily shopping rituals must have been therapeutic excursions away from motherhood. When I feel a need to get away from the trials of motherhood, sometimes I may read for a couple of hours. After taking this brief leave, I often come back ready to spend time with my children again.

I once asked my children about their enduring memories from earlier years. Their answers were not the expensive toys or vacations they had—but the time that we shared together. They remember the stories I read to them, an occasion when we met with my daughter's teacher at her new school, the conversations I shared with them. Had I known that quality time holds a higher value in my children's hearts than material things, I would have saved myself some money! Time spent with children is the best investment in the parent-child relationship. Physically and mentally exhausted parents are poor candidates for spending quality time with their children. To recharge yourself, regular breaks from parenthood are necessary.

It is heartwarming to know that time I spent with my children has a place in their memories. They do not place excessive value on material things. It has been my concern that being raised in America, a society of abundance, they would lose sight of what really matters in life. Although the United States enjoys a large portion of the world's bounty, I do not believe that children are entitled to indulge in excess—for example, buying exorbitantly expensive brand-name products. I often restrain myself from overindulging my teenagers, who are expected to stay within their clothing allowance. As a result, my daughters have learned to make choices about how to use their limited resources, to differentiate between needs and wants, to work with a budget, and to experience the pleasure of their own success in the endeavor. They may not always have what they want, but they are happy with what they have. They know that happiness has nothing to do with expensive possessions. They also gain confidence from the experience of successful money management.

As a parent, I have a responsibility to nurture confidence, provide guidance, and prepare my daughters and my son for the "real" world. In the real world, resources are limited, choices have consequences, and living within one's means is necessary. If I am to fulfill my goal of raising happy adults, I need to prepare them to deal with life's realities in childhood. Overindulgence during childhood creates false expectations for life. When such expectations are not met in adulthood, unhappiness results. Children become happy adults when they set realistic expectations and meet or exceed them. Happiness is a product of meeting one's own expectations.

During my children's early years, I enjoyed high status in their eyes. I was their authority, confidante, and object of affection. They showered me with their attention, hugs, and kisses, and they always wanted to sit on my lap. I considered these endearments some of the greatest pleasures of motherhood. As my children grew, however, they began to exert their independence and my status underwent a gradual decline. My once absolute authority was challenged, my position as confidante was usurped by friends, and their once abundant expressions of affection became less frequent. My only consolation was that my status as mother was still important to my young son.

Then, two years ago, I went on my son's school field trip as a parent volunteer. I scheduled the day off, thinking it would be a special time for us. Much to my dismay, my son was quick to inform me of some of his ground rules for how to behave properly during the trip. I was not to hug or kiss him in front of his friends and never to call him affectionate names, such as "honey." I went into defensive mode.

"If you keep this up," I threatened him, "when you're in college, I am going to introduce myself to your friends as your girlfriend, not your mother."

"Mom, do you remember how old you are?" my son asked, obviously unimpressed.

This is the boy who wanted to marry me just a few short years ago! He is also my youngest child. I must face the reality that the honeymoon stage with my children is gone forever; they no longer depend on my approval. They are well on their way toward independence. Given that raising independent children has been my goal, why am I reluctant to accept the facts? The irony is, as much as I want my children to be independent, I dislike having to move out of center stage in their lives. Who likes to become less important? Despite my reluctance, I nevertheless accept my diminishing role in my children's life. Like it or not, parenthood is a job with the goal of making itself obsolete. That is its nature.

A few days ago, I had a conversation with my older daughter about her future.

"I don't know if I want to have children. There is so much I want to do. I don't want to do it if I can't do a good job," my daughter said. My younger daughter has told me similar things. Although I have cautioned both my daughters that it is far too early for them to make decisions on this subject, I respect their reasoning.

Becoming a parent is making a commitment to do whatever is necessary to nurture a human being from infancy to adulthood. This commitment has a minimum duration of eighteen years, without the possibility of divorce or early release for good behavior. There is also the financial aspect, which I do not wish to tackle here.

Given the scope of the commitment and the importance of the task, I believe that having children needs to be a conscious decision. Raising children is too important to leave it up to chance. There are few tragedies greater than bringing an unwanted child into this world. I urge you to make parenthood a deliberate choice. Wait until you are emotionally and financially ready to have a child. The birth of a baby is an event to be celebrated. Parenthood has great consequences.

To quote Abraham Lincoln, "A child is a person who is going to carry on what you have started. They are going to sit where you are sitting, attend to those things which you think are important—the fate of humanity is in their hands."

After seventeen years of motherhood, I can safely call myself a veteran parent. I have developed a respect for all parents. I understand the work, the commitment, the challenges that parents face daily. Generation after generation we perform our task, sometimes with measurable success, sometimes not. Can success be measured? I think not. My children have their strengths and shortcomings—they are not perfect by any means—no surprise there. They have been raised by an imperfect me, with single parent-hood to top that in recent years. My daughters and my son have different dreams and aspirations from my own. I cannot measure them against my own model. I only want them to be good people. I wish for their happiness. My children should have the freedom to choose the lives they want to lead. I have concluded that there is no uniform measure for success in parenting. As long as our children turn out to be good people, we parents have done our job. No matter what our children's achievements are, there is but one certainty in parenthood: Parents commit themselves to parenthood out of love for their children.

My dear daughter, parenthood is the most important job in life, for our children are our future. Choose your parenting techniques wisely. Commit yourself to good parenting by continuous education and self-improvement. Be prepared to satisfy your children's needs before your own. Parenthood has the power to transform you—to help you become a better person. Spend time with your children, for they cherish quality time with you. Take time off to revitalize yourself. Realize that your parental responsibilities include providing guidance, instilling values, and nurturing confidence. Implement actions to fulfill them. Make parenthood a choice. Your children deserve to be wanted. That, I promise, will enhance your life as a parent.

Friendship

友情

In memory of my friend Alice Chan

One sweltering summer evening in 1998, I received a phone call from my sister Norma, who lives in Toronto.

"Your old college friend Vic was looking for you. He's in Toronto for a few days to check on his condo. Do you know Alice passed away?"

"What? No, that can't be true!" I cried. "Are you sure? When? Where?"

"April. In Ottawa," my sister continued, "Vic said he just found out himself. He stopped by Ottawa and called Alice to have lunch or something. Her son told him. She died of cancer."

"Oh no! I can't believe it. That's unreal!" I said, in shock.

Alice was my best friend during the early college days before my marriage. Through the years when my husband and I were moving around the United States she lived in Ottawa, but we never failed to keep in touch with each other. Besides sending Christmas greeting cards, I would call her from time to time during my yearly visit to my family in Toronto. I always promised her that I would come to Ottawa on my next trip to Canada.

"Yeah, I'll see you after my hair turns gray," Alice said to me during our last phone conversation, more than two years ago. I never doubted that we would see each other again. There was always tomorrow—another chance for a visit. Then came the shattering news of her death.

For a good ten minutes after my phone conversation with my sister, I sat motionless, having trouble gathering my thoughts. My heart was aching. The first thing I did after getting up from the chair was to take my dusty old photo albums off the shelf. I wanted to find Alice's face again.

Looking through old photographs of us together opened the floodgate of tears. With blurred eyes, I looked at the images of Alice, myself, and friends from long ago. We were not quite adults then, smiling and laughing in youthful innocence. There we were, standing in front of a vibrant tulip bed one early spring day; posing with Niagara Falls in the background during a summer trip; drinking tea at her parents' house after a stroll in Canadian maple woods one crimson and golden autumn day; throwing snowballs at each other in the winter chill. We spent a lot of time together—dreaming the future, exchanging stories, sharing secrets, and venting problems.

We had a habit of taking walks together to discuss problems, mostly about our boyfriends. For a while, both our boyfriends lived in the same dorm building. Alice and I often walked in the park near the shortcut to their dormitory. As we were leaving the park one day, Alice stopped and gazed into the distance.

"What are you doing?" I asked.

"You know, this is our park," she said to me. "When we're old ladies, we'll still be walking around here and talking to each other about our secrets and problems."

"But we won't be talking about boyfriend problems. Can you imagine two little old ladies talking about boyfriends?" I said.

"We'll be talking about our husbands, kids, grandkids, and my dog!" she replied. I thought that we would walk in the park together in old age. I did not expect that my friend's life would be cut short. Nothing prepared me for that. It was difficult to accept the fact that I would never see her again. Death is so final.

I wish that I had done a better job of keeping in touch with Alice. I moved to the United States after my marriage. Two years later I went to her wedding, then we saw each other only four or five times in the next twenty years. In the beginning, we exchanged letters and phone calls frequently. But as the years went by, I became less and less diligent in answering letters. In the last ten years, our letters dwindled to one or two a year, but she never missed sending Christmas cards to me, except in the last year of her life. For my part, however, I only sent occasional Christmas greetings. We kept each other informed about our lives through occasional phone calls. Whenever we talked on the phone, it was as if we were back in the old days. We still addressed each other by our nicknames, and giggled at each other's jokes and silly remarks. The passing years and geographic distance did not seem to affect the way we related to each other. We were still two girls—young at heart—sharing our souls.

Of all my old friends, Alice was the only one who always knew where to find me as I moved frequently during the first ten years of my marriage. I never failed to inform her of my new address. She was the one whom my old friends went to when they wanted to contact me. Everyone from our old social circle knew that we were best friends. Now, I wondered why I had not been informed of her passing.

I called Alice's husband, Tom. He was still grieving for her.

"Why wasn't I told?" I asked, desperate to know.

"She didn't want to tell anyone, not even her brothers and sister," Tom said. "They didn't know about this until the last week."

"Why didn't you tell me then?" I asked.

"She didn't want me to tell," he explained. "She didn't want pity. She's a private person, you know."

"Not even me?" I asked, even though I knew that it had to be true. I knew Alice well.

"I wanted to call you. I know you guys were best friends. But she wouldn't let me. She'd finished chemo then. She didn't want you to see her like that." He went on, "I looked for your phone number afterwards, but couldn't find it. I don't know where she put it."

So my friend chose to fight her battle privately. I would have liked to be with her, doing what I could, making her struggle a little easier. At the same time, I wished that I had called or written her while she was fighting for her life. I even failed to notice how peculiar it was that I had not received her annual Christmas card. I had taken our friendship for granted, never expecting to lose it to cancer.

"I'll come visit her grave," I told Tom.

I shall keep my promise this time. I want to tell Alice that I will never forget her. And I want to bring her two sons to our park, to tell them about their mother's youth and what a lovely young woman she was. I want them to know that her friendship was one of the blessings in my life. She will always have a place in my heart.

My friend Vic lives in Asia. I think of him as someone with whom I had some memorable outings. One was an impromptu trip to Niagara Falls—with my sister and his brother—in a $250 car that he had purchased the day before. The car promptly broke down after we arrived in Niagara Falls. We ended up riding back to Toronto behind a tow truck.

Then there was our tour of Wildlife Safari with Vic, his best friend, my sister, and me, in a car borrowed from his friend's parents. By the end of the tour, the car's side mirror had been appropriated by a hungry black bear, and a troupe of mischievous monkeys had removed some of the chrome strips. I never found out how his best friend's parents reacted.

Vic and I have kept in touch despite the fact that we never seem to have each other's addresses and phone numbers. With my numerous moves in the States, and his moves among Canada, New Zealand, and Asia, we were never sure of each other's whereabouts. Miraculously, we always managed to find each other through our families. Whenever he was in Toronto, he would call my sister to find out if I was in town. Although we never arranged our meetings in advance, we saw each other every few years in Toronto.

After my sister Norma told me about Vic's call, I called his brother in Toronto and left a message for him to call me in Oregon. When he did, we mourned Alice's passing—still in disbelief.

"I actually called her to get together last time I was in Ottawa," he said, "but she couldn't make it. So I thought we'd do it this time. Who would have guessed?"

"I didn't expect that either. She was still young. It's not supposed to be like that!" I said.

"Judy, we must keep in touch," he said. "We'll always value our friendship."

Yes, I know that we will. We are two people taking separate life voyages, passing from time to time on the open sea. When we meet, we are always delighted to see each other. Our friendship has survived the tests of time, distance, and inattention. It is meant to last a lifetime.

Before settling in Oregon, I lived in Tacoma, Washington for four years—the longest I had lived in one place since moving to the States. I made many friends there. Some of them have become very important people in my life.

One evening last week, my friend Darlene called from Tacoma to tell me that there was a documentary about Chinese-Americans on public TV that evening. We ended up chatting for a whole hour until the program came on.

"Before we go, I need to tell you this," I said. "I told my photographer I wanted her to make me look good in the picture. She said, 'Wait a minute, I'm not a magician!'"

"Oh, Judy, you'll look lovely. You always do," Darlene said, laughing out loud.

That is Darlene, always having kind words for me.

"Must let you go so you can watch. I'll go check the program guide," I said.

"I'll tape the program for you. Just in case you don't get it," she answered.

That is Darlene, always watching out for me.

I met Darlene on Halloween in 1984, shortly after I moved to Tacoma. I opened my front door to greet trick-or-treaters, and there stood a tall blonde woman with sparkling blue eyes, shepherding her two-year-old son. She introduced herself as my neighbor from across the street. She too had just moved to Tacoma. Her warm smile and kind demeanor instantly made me want to be her friend. Her son, Austin, and my daughter, Venus, were the same age, so we saw each other frequently while I was in Tacoma. I got to know her husband, Rob, and their older son, Chris, as well; she got to know my family. Our friendship was bonded by similar values and tastes, a shared interest in good books, and mutual respect.

After I moved to Oregon, we continued to see each other once every couple of months. We often met at a restaurant just off the I-5 freeway, halfway between our homes. I suspect that the restaurant was there for no other reason than our meetings. The waitress even remembered us. We left home after our children had gone to school in the morning and met each other an hour or so later. Over breakfast and two pots of tea, we spent the next few hours sharing our thoughts and stories, confiding our joy, pain, and fear, exchanging advice and opinions. The sound of our chatter, giggles, and occasional roars of laughter filtered through the air of the café. For me, those were hours of comfort and warmth, basking in the radiance of a wonderful friendship.

"I can't think of any other friend who'd drive more than an hour just to see what I wrote," I told her one day. She has read and reviewed my whole manuscript of this book. Her feedback, suggestions, and encouragement have been invaluable to me.

In the fifteen years since Darlene and I first met she has seen me through deep joy—such as the birth of my second daughter, Amanda, and my son, Nathan—and through the great sorrow of my divorce. She never failed to cheer for my happiness or to offer kind words and encouragement in my despair. She was always ready to lend an ear when I needed to talk. I watched her devote the same good nature and tireless effort to promoting cultural diversity and literacy in her community. She is responsible for engineering a cultural diversity program for her school district, teaching, and developing teachers' materials and training programs for the literacy council.

One Saturday last fall, Darlene and Rob took two of her students, immigrants from Russia, to Portland for a one-day visit. I seized the opportunity to spend the day with them. In a Northwest autumn drizzle, we took a walking tour of downtown Portland. Her students were thrilled to play tourists for the day, away from their struggle to adapt to a new country. I watched my friend shower her students with kindness.

Later, she sent me an e-mail about a thank-you card she had received from some of her other students. "I had the three Latvian students here for dessert, coffee, and conversation last week and received the loveliest, heartfelt thank you yesterday—both for the occasion and for the time I have given them. The catch is that it was written inside a sympathy card! I am so tickled (and touched by their kind words and dear effort!) but, as their teacher, I feel I must think of some way to gently talk to them about it."

Humor, kindness, and commitment in service to others are only some of the many admirable qualities of this intelligent and compassionate woman, whom I am proud to call my dear friend.

Living in Tacoma with two preschool children, thousands of miles away from my parents and sisters, I depended on my friends to keep me in touch with the adult world. Three of those women, who live in different parts of the country today, have enriched my life in many ways. Although I cannot see them as often as I used to, my relationships with them are among my life's treasures.

Forsythias blossoming in spring always remind me of Dawna, who now lives in Nebraska. I vividly recall one clear spring day in 1986. Standing on my front lawn touching the forsythia flowers, she told me that these shrubs were everywhere during her New England childhood. That moment is forever captured in my memory, like a snapshot.

Dawna and I were members of the executive board of the private preschool attended by her son, Jason, and my daughter Venus. We developed a close working and personal relationship during that school year. She was the person who inspired me to explore my artistic side. We went to a toy party together and bought some unfinished wooden toys for our children. I was debating how to finish the wood surface when she offered to lend me her acrylic painting supplies. She showed me the basic techniques of using acrylic media. Although I had never tried acrylic painting before, I enjoyed the opportunity. I knew that I could draw—as a child I drew constantly—but I had not done any drawing in years. Using Dawna's supplies, I decorated the wooden toys. Rediscovering the pleasure of drawing and experimenting with acrylic paints for the first time led to my adopting the hobby of watercolor painting.

After Dawna left Tacoma in 1986, we kept in touch through occasional phone calls and letters. Now, we correspond mostly by e-mail. I have always respected Dawna's intelligent, analytical mind. I have sought advice from her on many occasions. She always had time for me whenever I wanted to talk. When I was thinking of returning to the work force, she suggested that I combine my language skills and business education. As it turned out, I now use both. I sent her the first draft of my opening letter of this book to critique, and she e-mailed me her feedback.

"Try to break up your paragraphs, making them shorter and easier to read," Dawna wrote. "Your reader may have bifocals (like me), so give their eyes some breathing room!"

Dawna's critique exemplified her direct, no-nonsense approach and sense of humor. I love her for that.

A few months ago, I received a package. It was from my friend Paula, who lives in Virginia.

"It's the book with her quilt in it!" I gasped, as I removed the wrapping. Sure enough, it was *Quilting with Manhole Covers: A Treasure Trove of Unique Designs from the Streets of Japan.* I had inquired about this book when I found out that a quilt she had made was in it. My intention was to look for it in local bookstores. I did not expect to get it as a gift with a nice inscription from her. But that is Paula, always generous with her friends.

I learned from Paula to appreciate the art of quilting. Before I met her more than thirteen years ago, I knew absolutely nothing about this traditional American art form. Seeing her work for the first time, I was captivated by the beauty that she created from ordinary fabric. I found out that quilting was her passion, and she was good at other crafts as well. Besides two of Paula's beautiful original quilts adorning the walls of my home, I also have a Christmas reindeer and an Easter bunny she made for me.

When I first met Paula, she, like I, had two preschool children. My two daughters, Venus and Amanda, were the same age as her daughter, Katie, and her son, Jeffrey. Paula and I did many things together, with and without our children. In addition to our children's play group and other activities, we met at our book group, recipe club, and many outings. I felt a special closeness with her. We had common bonds—we were at the same stage of our lives, both choosing family over career but wanting to have a life beyond motherhood.

One spring day, I went to the fabric store with Paula to get materials for making Easter bunnies. She was going to make three: one for herself, one for her mother, and one for me. Within two days, her husband, Terry, brought me the adorable bunny that she had made. She had managed to finish the bunny-making along with all the other activities in her busy life.

"Oh, so quick! She works fast!" I was impressed.

Paula inspires. She is the kind of person who makes things happen, and quickly. There were always new projects and she accomplished them with ease. At the same time, she rallied her friends to explore new territory. When I took up watercolor painting, she was there to cheer me on. It was no different when I informed her that I was writing this book. She offered support and encouragement, as always. I am fortunate to claim her as a friend—an intelligent, dynamic woman who manages her family, art, responsibilities, and community service with uncommon grace.

Paula and I both left Tacoma in 1988. Today, we maintain a regular e-mail correspondence, keeping each other informed about our lives. She has taken her quilting further since we parted. Besides staying active with quilters' groups, she designs quilts and teaches the art. Her quilts appear on the Web and in books and magazines, and they have been displayed on the East coast.

In late 1987, another friend, Linda, suggested that I take a watercolor painting class with her. Linda is a talented amateur artist. When I saw her marvelous paintings, I expressed a desire to realize my drawings in paint. I was surprised and honored when she invited me to join her painting class. It was the most delightful class that I had ever taken, largely because of Linda's presence. She made me laugh. Because of the students' different skill levels, our teacher let us choose our own subjects to paint, offering assistance when needed. We painted, joked, and chatted in class for three hours twice a week. Linda constantly encouraged me. We also got together at home, for painting sessions. Thus I discovered one of the greatest pleasures that I have ever known.

Linda is one of the funniest and most talented people I know. Her work is not limited to painting; she is always creating things. I had so much admiration for her when I discovered that all the ornaments on her family's Christmas tree were her own creations. In spite of her enormous talents, however, Linda did not take her art seriously.

"You should get your paintings framed. They're gorgeous!" I said to her more than once. I wanted to see her paintings on display, not filed away. Thinking she was good enough to be a teacher, I asked why she wanted to take classes continuously.

"I use that time to paint. If I don't go to a class, I usually don't set aside the time to paint," she said to me.

That is Linda—talented, low-key, always delightful to be with. With all her artistry, she remains foremost a wife and mother. Now that I have moved to Oregon we cannot go to painting classes together anymore, but we stay in touch by e-mail. I cherish the hope that someday, somewhere, somehow, I will paint with my friend again.

When I first moved to Oregon I did not know a soul there, but I have since made many friends. A few of them sustained me through great changes in my life. Their friendship brightened my life's passage.

Cornelia and her husband Dale are two people who saw me through the worst of times—my divorce. They offered me their home when I needed a place to go, their time when I needed to talk, and their advice when I needed to hear it. In the past few years, my children and I have been invited to Thanksgiving, Christmas, and New Year's dinners with their family. It was a great comfort to have a family to go to while my own was breaking up.

I met Cornelia shortly after I arrived in Oregon. Our daughters were in the same class. In our more than ten years of friendship, we have seen each other through the best of times and the worst of times. Her divorce; her second marriage, to Dale; the birth of my son; my divorce—all were woven into the tapestry of our friendship. We shared our joy with laughter and warm embraces, and our sorrow with tears and consolation.

Flora is another friend whom I met through our daughters' school. We were both wives and mothers, school volunteers, and friends to each other. Then both our lives took a turn in the same direction. We both went through divorces at about the same time. Now that we have returned to the work force, juggling single parenthood and our various work-related activities, we do not see each other often. Once every few months, though, we make time to meet and update each other about our lives. We listen, advise, and show that we care. The circumstances of our lives have changed, but our friendship lives on.

When my friend Lisa lived in Oregon, we went to see art films together. She was very interested in movies and took a film critique course at our community college. I enjoyed hearing her talk about them. We saw each other often. My son, Nathan, and her daughter Amy are the same age. Together we started a recipe club and joined the American Association of University Women. Since Lisa moved to Colorado a few years ago, we have only seen each other twice. She came back to Oregon for a visit a year after her move. Then my family went to Colorado for a week of skiing, and we got together near the ski resort. We have stayed in touch and I know that we always will.

One glorious summer evening a few months ago, a group of my friends and I got together to review my book. When they first suggested this session, I hesitated for a moment. As a first-time writer, with shaky confidence, I was somewhat apprehensive. However, I wanted to get input from people I respect and value.

"Bring everything with you. We're going to grill you," my friend Annette e-mailed me the day before.

Armed with my manuscript, I put up a brave front to face the music. I had no idea what to expect. After food, drinks, and lots of fun and lively conversation, we got down to business. My friends Annette, Arloa, and Diane read my chapter out loud as their husbands, Royce, Jim, and Art, and I listened. Hearing someone read my book was a foreign feeling. Listening to my own words gave me a different perspective on my writing. I truly appreciated the opportunity to have my work critiqued. Looking at the circle of friends around me, I realized how fortunate I was to be surrounded by them. They are my support system of cherished friends.

Whenever I think of my circles of friends, I think of my sisters Norma, Maria, Irene, and Kathy, as well. I consider my sisters my best friends. We trust and confide in one another. We offer support, advice, and reassuring love. Friends of past and present, near and far, are people I hold dear. Their presence brings warmth and beauty to everyday living. A walk with Karen, or a phone conversation with Catherine, or lunch with Marylu brightens up my day. I am grateful for my friends. I count their friendship among my life's blessings.

My dear daughter, friends are important people in life. Select your friends with care. Treasure them. Reciprocate the gift of friendship. May you be blessed with circles of loving friends. Celebrate the sweetness of friendship. That, I promise, will contribute to your happiness.

Part II

From
Family and Friends

Special thanks to all contributing authors for generously sharing their thoughts and insights. I am honored to have their writings grace this book.

Ursula Bacon
Stephen Barkley
Bob Barrett
Darlene Flack
Paula Golden
Terry Golden
Diane Hansen
Katherine Kan
Dawna Robertson
Arloa Christiansen-Sambol
Linda Sanker
Lisa Snella
Annette Young
Royce Young

Essays from Family and Friends

As my niece approaches her eighteenth birthday, she is soon to be catapulted into the adventures of university, with the possibility of experiencing true freedom for the first time in her life. It is making me reflect on the glorious years of my own exciting youth. The journey that has transformed me from an insecure, rebellious teenager into a content, confident woman has been full of trials and well-learned lessons. It has been a transformation from the seeming immortality of youth to the realization of the mortality of being human. I would like to share a few personal views from my own life's excursion to date.

♦ Self-respect and confidence are the most important attributes any individual possesses. Without self-love and worth, how can you convince others you deserve their love and consideration? Let's face it, no one will ever spend more time with you than yourself. In order for that relationship to succeed, self-admiration has to be a top priority. Don't you agree?

♦ Exercise your own voice and mind: be true to yourself. Nonconformity to society's ideas and norms is completely acceptable. This does not mean becoming a delinquent, but rather proceeding in life with your own beliefs. Too often others try to influence how one should handle certain situations, which direction to take, what is the best advice, and so on, based on their own opinions. (Ironically, here I am putting in my own two cents' worth!) Although motivated purely by concern and love, people tend to forget it is not their place to dictate another's action or choice. If an individual errs—and we all do—so be it. Mistakes are valuable lessons and not necessarily bad; they are an aid to growth.

♦ Take time out to help others less fortunate; show compassion. Many of us tend to take for granted the day-to-day fundamentals, such as eating, having shelter, and being healthy, protected, and loved by family and friends. Many people, however, are not so fortunate. Whenever it is possible and within your means, be kind to others, share your time, give blood, deliver meals on wheels, listen with your ears and act with your heart, and if possible share some of your wealth. Sometimes even the smallest contribution can make the biggest impact on someone else's life.

♦ Have a good sense of humor; laugh at yourself and all circumstances. Certain situations will seem disastrous at the time, but like everything else in life, their level of severity will change with time. Adopt the perspective of a third party with a sense of humor, and I guarantee that you will have a good chuckle.

♦ Live life! Do not just exist. Do what you want to do; embrace new experiences and ideas; travel. Enrich your mind and soul as often as possible. Structure your life so that you will be glad you did things, and not wish you had.

This is an exciting and liberating time to be a woman. The opportunities presented to us today that evaded our mothers are boundless. Fasten your seat belt, because it is going to be a wild and wonderful ride!

KATHERINE KAN

My mother told me that it was my good fortune to have been raised on three continents, despite the extraordinarily difficult circumstances that prevailed during those terribly trying times from 1933 to 1945. She insisted that I—a child in Germany, an adolescent in China, and an adult in America—had learned a great deal more about the different ways people act in their own corners of the world than I would have if I had I stayed in one place.

She talked about the unique formality of the traditional Chinese family, the tightly closed ranks of the sometimes overly protective Jewish household, and the sometimes vague casual nature of the French family unit. But mostly she talked about respect. She was emphatic as she pointed out that respect was the single universal quality that represented and preserved the very foundation of civilization.

"Respect yourself, respect the world." She has long passed on, but I can still hear her say these words.

As I grew older, I came to realize just how true was her appraisal of life and how sound her wisdom. Respect is everything. Truly, it is.

When we respect ourselves—our body, our mind, and our spirit—we think twice before doing something that would harm us. When we respect ourselves, we automatically respect our fellow human beings and all other living things. We become sensitive to people's feelings, and whether we agree with them or not, we respect their right to express themselves.

"If we had enough respect for each other across and around the globe," Mother said, "there would be no wars. What do you think about that?" she challenged me.

Respect is a constant practice, most rewarding and totally satisfying as we experience life. Respect is magic: it breeds love, and love breeds grace, and grace is the gift we give to others as well as to ourselves.

Respect! Don't leave home without it.

URSULA BACON

The older I get, the more I realize how much of a mystery life is, and how much I really do not understand. Jesus talked about this in one of his parables when he said that to have life, you must first lose it—something I have experienced only a few times. The reason these experiences stand out so clearly against the backdrop of the rest of my life is, I believe, because those were the times I was experiencing life more fully—when I actually was able to give more of myself away, without expecting anything in return.

My first experience happened when I had the opportunity to live in Japan for two years, teaching English and helping in a Christian church there. I can still feel the frustration of not being able to communicate with most of the people around me, and my motivation to learn the language and customs of Japan. The awareness that I had something they wanted— good English pronunciation—was amazing to me, and I strove to meet their need and give all I had, to truly be their friend. This experience was a building block for my second experience.

After returning from Japan, I was suddenly faced with the great need of the refugees who had recently arrived from Southeast Asia. With my own experience in Japan fresh in my heart, I had such immediate love and patience with these people who were strangers in our land that I knew God had prepared me through my own time in Japan. For most of the next decade I found life's greatest reward in helping these people and giving of myself in ways that were far greater than I thought I could. It was a life-changing experience and one where the rewards were mine because of the invaluable lessons I learned and the love I received.

Not everyone has the opportunity to live in another culture or work with people in such dire circumstances, but every day we have small opportunities that can make a difference. We are all gifted in different ways that make us unique, but the secret, I believe, lies in the ability to go beyond our fears and imposed limitations to reach for a higher calling that is outside ourselves—to see ourselves as a vessel to be used by God to touch the lives of others in whatever place we find ourselves. Life truly is a mystery, but the exciting part is that we all have the key within us to open life's door.

DIANE HANSEN

Money is the root of all evil. Or, money is the key to your future. Or, money is the entire focus of your life. All these statements are comments about finance. They may be true, or they may be false. In my years as a certified public accountant, I have learned that money is nothing more than a tool, just like a shovel or a rake. Used properly, it can better your life and make your toil easier. However, used improperly, it can burden you with problems that only increase with time. Following are some thoughts and suggestions for young people just starting out in life about how to deal with the temptations of money and finance. Just remember that ultimately it is your decision whether you control your finances, or whether your finances control you.

There are many forms of money: cash, debit and credit cards, savings and investment accounts, checking accounts, liquid and nonliquid assets, mortgages, lines of credit, and a hundred others. When you start out in life, you typically have a clean slate: that is, you are usually debt-free.

For the few who plan ahead, these early years provide an opportunity to get ahead and stay there. Most young people have some sort of income by the time they graduate from high school. This is the time to learn to live by the axiom "Live within your means." This does not mean spending every dime of your paycheck. Living within your means should include setting aside 10 to 20 percent of your take-home pay for big purchases such as furniture for the first apartment or a new car. Teaching yourself not to spend every dime you bring home is, in my opinion, one of the most important steps toward financial success in life. When you have uncommitted funds accumulating, you open yourself to numerous opportunities. If you have lived this way, you can take that dream job that starts out at a lower pay level; you have money set aside to pay for specialized education. You have freedom.

This freedom will allow you to explore your life desires and seek out the real you: who you want to be, where you want to live, the career path you want to follow. Without this freedom, life becomes a daily exercise in survival rather than an adventure in discovery. You end up needing to go to work rather than wanting to go to work. I once heard someone say what a shame it was that most people look forward to the weekend when, in fact, they spend only two days in their weekend and five days in their work week. Wouldn't it be great to awaken each morning and be excited about going to work?

Now, how do we go about attaining this freedom? The number one killer of freedom in our society today is the misuse of debt. As we travel on this journey called life, many of us seek to satisfy our desires for new things by borrowing the money to acquire them. We then are in debt and are forced to work to service the debt in order to keep and enjoy the things with which we have surrounded ourselves.

Debt is a tool that is easily abused. It is not unusual to meet people who owe two to three times their annual income, not even including a home mortgage. Needless to say, their consumption has far outstripped their ability to pay. They spend the next six to ten years trying to pay off the debt they accumulated while still trying to maintain the lifestyle they couldn't afford in the first place.

The consequences of this can be disastrous. Bankruptcy and credit counseling are only the tip of the iceberg when we measure the cost of this misspending. The missed opportunities and emotional turmoil are the true harm to many of those who are deep in debt. They can't afford to take that dream job because the starting pay won't cover their bills. They can't afford their lifestyle and blame their partner, then end up in divorce or worse because of their inability to discipline themselves by saying "no" to their desires.

Debt is not bad in and of itself. The problem is that we can finance almost anything with debt now. You've seen the offers for low-interest credit cards and no interest for a year. However, if you use these tools to buy consumer goods, you are using debt to purchase something that will not be worth the level of debt you assumed one day after you bring it home. To add insult to injury, you not only owe the debt; the interest typically accrues at 18 to 22 percent annually, so the true cost of your purchase, by the time you make all the payments, can be two to three times the purchase price.

For those who say it is important to use debt to establish your credit, I say, "Go buy a car." This is the simplest way to establish credit, and you will have something tangible and, in today's mobile world, necessary to use while establishing your credit. Furthermore, the interest rate on an auto loan is typically 8 to 12 percent, a much lower rate than most credit cards. You will train yourself in the discipline of making payments, too. Just remember that the loan payment is only part of the monthly cost of owning an automobile. You need to put money aside for insurance, gas, oil, and maintenance. It is also important to have a fund for replacement items such as tires and brakes.

Debt can be a wonderful thing, but it can have dire consequences. For myself, I have tried to engineer my life so that the only times I use debt are (a) in an emergency situation, (b) for a big-ticket purchase such as a house or car, and (c) to purchase items that I believe will increase in value. I try not to use debt to purchase things with no tangible value, like a dinner or vacation, unless I am absolutely certain I can pay off the debt as soon as the bill comes.

Now that we know how bad debt can harm us, let's talk about the fun side of money. Saving and investing can be both fun and rewarding. How can this be, you ask? Let me tell you.

Every person should establish a pattern of saving as soon as possible. We've all heard that, but why should we? Because of the greatest weapon in our financial arsenal: time. I believe it was J. Paul Getty who once said that compound interest is the eighth wonder of the world. For the simple act of not spending our money today, we are paid interest on it. Tomorrow, we are paid interest on our money plus the interest we earned yesterday. Cool! We get paid to do nothing!

When we save money, we are expanding our future opportunities. When we spend money today, we have forgone numerous opportunities in the unseen future. For example, while in college a friend and I bought shares of Nike stock at $9 a share. Within the year, the stock moved to $18, and we sold our shares to get money for a party. Foolish decision! Had we held the stock until today, we would both have enough money for a significant down payment on our dream homes, or some other more valuable expenditure. We allowed our need for immediate gratification to sabotage our savings discipline. People do this every day. They use their desire for a bigger TV or a sports car as an excuse to sabotage their savings.

Saving today is simpler than ever. Most mutual funds say that they want a minimum initial deposit of $1,000 to $3,000. What most don't advertise is that if you are willing to commit to an automatic withdrawal from your checking or savings bank account, they will open the account with no initial deposit. The minimum monthly deposit is usually $25 to $50. If a young person commits herself to a mere $25 a month in a mutual fund and sticks with it for ten years, she will have accumulated $5,163.80 if the fund earns 10 percent, and $6,966.43 if it earns 15 percent. Not bad, when you consider that she contributed only $3,000. This would be a great head start on her children's education.

Some additional food for thought: If she continued to save the $25 a month from age eighteen through age sixty-five and earned 10 percent, she would have a savings account valued at $323,250.60 for a total contribution of $14,100. If she begins at age 28, her savings total would be $117,644.54. Obviously, waiting can seriously reduce your accumulation. This is why I preach that your biggest weapon is time. By waiting ten years, you not only lose 10 years of deposits; you also lose forty-seven years of interest on the skipped ten years' deposits.

Think about the last paragraph, and then consider this. We now have a savings vehicle called a "Roth IRA." Although the contribution to a Roth IRA is not deductible for tax purposes, none of the money earned by the arrangement is ever taxed. Let me say this again, because it is very important: *the earnings in the Roth IRA are never taxed.* Anytime you can earn tax-free money, you need to consider doing so.

Going back to my example of saving $25 a month, let's say you earn $1,000 a month. After taxes, you would take home approximately $10,366 a year or $864 a month. $25 a month represents 2.9 percent of your take-home pay. Many experts say you should try to save 5 to 10 percent of your take-home pay. Now imagine that we move forward twenty years. Now you're thirty-eight and you are making a modest $50,000 a year. You are still single. After taxes, your take-home pay is about $3,000 a month. Your $25 a month is now only 0.8 percent of your take-home pay. Obviously, this is a drop in the bucket, yet it can add significantly to your comfort as you reach your later years. It can even make the difference between early retirement or working until age sixty-five.

I could go on and on, but let me just make a few key points as you set out on your financial life.

♦ Be a saver. The emotional contentment, access to opportunity, and safety from uncertainty will enable you to lead a much fuller life than you would otherwise.

♦ Use debt carefully. Once you let this dragon out of its cave, it is extremely hard to chase it back in. There is a time and place to use debt; just make sure you think before you spend on credit.

♦ Use the weapon of time wisely. If you save only 3 percent of your income during your lifetime, but save it continuously, you will have an accumulation of wealth to provide you with the freedom we all seek.

For more information about money and finance, seek the help of a qualified financial professional.

Check their credentials. Read books about money and finance. Observe your friends and don't make the same mistakes they make. In short, take control of your financial life, and don't let others deflect you from achieving your dreams and goals.

STEPHEN L. BARKLEY, CPA

My mother has funny quirks. I notice them now, but growing up, I just assumed things were done this way or that, never questioning her motivation. For instance, my mother has strong notions on how to dry and store the dishes. "Never place the glasses upside down on the shelf," she says, "and it's always best to let the dishes air-dry by themselves."

She was always adamant where her rules on kitchen hygiene were concerned. Most people can follow the reasoning about air-drying the dishes to reduce the spread of germs. Mom was the daughter of a country doctor, so I could understand where she picked up this idea. Nonetheless, she freely admits to being a "clean nut" in her adherence to all the other rules of the kitchen. The part about the upturned glasses always puzzled me. Growing up, I noticed that *everyone* except us stored their glasses upside down in the cupboard. Yet, miraculously, the upside-down families seemed to thrive, despite this transgression. Later, as a nursing student, I sought to discover a single instance where a family became sick or died as a result of upside-down tumblers; it never happened. Years later, I questioned my mother on this fine point. She had on an apron and rubber gloves—items I kept for her annual visits, never using them myself. The water she used to rinse the dishes *before* they went into the dishwasher was scalding. I said, "I've never been able to figure you out, Mom. Germ theory I can grasp, but what's with the glasses right side up?"

She cocked her head with a little frown and paused. She was stumped! She saw the grin creeping across my face as I dismissed a truth she had long held dear. Well out of my teen years, I could still gain satisfaction by disproving a parental dictate.

"Polio," she said at last. "For the longest time, we had to worry about polio. I'm sure you don't remember. I have a lot of hang-ups from that time, you know."

How could I remember? I was born the very year a killed-virus vaccine first became available. But I remember vividly the excitement when the oral vaccine arrived. All the children in the school anxiously awaited vaccination, expecting a painful needle, only to be given a few odd-tasting drops in the mouth. Polio had been a dreaded scourge right up through the 1950s—not unlike the AIDS and hepatitis viruses we face today.

The polio vaccine was a major technological breakthrough, yet it is all but forgotten today. Indeed, people now take for granted the tremendous advances in medicine, technology, and social reform that have occurred in the past century. I believe the solutions have come so fast and so efficiently that people have developed unrealistically high expectations of government and industry, without pausing to reflect on the social impact these extraordinary developments have produced.

Consider that my parents' generation marched into World War II with almost no antibiotics. Or that the first astronauts who landed on the Moon did it without the benefit of the computer chip; would you blast off into space with a gigantic payload of computer hardware that couldn't perform with the complexity of today's laptop? When the Apollo 13 crew made their famous understatement, "Houston, we have a problem," their vulnerability was compounded by the fact that they were still relying on *slide rules*. I used a slide rule in high school; my teenage daughter insists this is proof that I was born in the Stone Age.

Just think: the routine ultrasound screenings that American women have come to rely on during pregnancy were little more than a *Star Trek* fantasy only twenty years ago. Twenty years ago, no one imagined that the Berlin Wall would be collectible fragments scattered worldwide in specialty stores. Women have had the right to vote for only eighty years, and Black Americans weren't truly emancipated until after the civil rights movement of the 1960s.

The pace of human progress in this century alone has been astounding, to say nothing of the past thousand years. So, as we turn a landmark corner on the Western calendar, ask yourself: Is the year 2000 just another year? Given that American culture tends to promote the new and disposable, it would be easy to dismiss Year 2000 as just another occasion for a frivolous New Year's party. However, civilized people the world over recognize that all achievement relies on the effort, experiences, and insights of those who came before us. Reverence for our ancestors and reflections on our history are not old-fashioned ideas: we *need* to be mindful of history's lessons for the sake of our collective future. Like the song says, "You can't know where you're going if you don't know where you are."

So is the year 2000 just another year? Without historical perspective, it is easy to dismiss this as just another date. What we must not lose sight of is that we are each a part of a bigger picture. Who we are today has everything to do with our past—our roots. Conversely, the meaningfulness we give to our lives today will have an effect on future generations. Is the year 2000 just another date? Not when we recognize and honor the ties we have to one another in the past, present, and future.

DAWNA L. ROBERTSON

There is still so much to learn that I wonder what I can offer. But living teaches. As our society has become farther spread apart, we have lost the wisdom of our elders that might have been shared on walks, around the dinner table, at family gatherings, or within the neighborhood—though if I had grown up in such a neighborhood, I doubt that I would have listened to them. I am one who has always had to do it my way and to learn the hard way. Experience does teach lessons, but if we don't learn the first time, the experiences get repeated over and over until we do.

I have become a quilter, and using fabric and threads to express important issues is my passion. As I have developed as a quilter, I have found that the lessons from life can be applied to creating, and vice versa. Here are some of the principles I've learned.

♦ There are no ugly fabrics. Everyone has a special gift to offer.

♦ Play! With play one becomes rejuvenated; the "shoulds" disappear, and time really does stand still. To be "in the moment" is to experience a bit of eternity.

♦ Do not give up on your ideals and dreams. Life can change perceptions from black and white to shades of gray, but right and wrong remain.

♦ Find a passion! If you can make this your life's work, then you will never be bored or lack for joy. Even if the financial benefits of your passion are pretty slim, you will always have joy.

♦ What goes around comes around. The smile, the gift of change to the person next to you in the checkout line, the cat you take in, the friend whose child you pick up from soccer practice—when you need help it will come from the most unexpected places, but it will be there.

♦ Love with your heart, soul, and passion. The gifts of love are that it has no boundaries, and that there is plenty to share.

♦ Work hard and luck will follow. Your reputation will blossom and good things will come to you.

♦ Invest early. My grandmother always said, "A third for rent, a third to save, and a third to live on." That seems a bit stringent for today, but if you always remember to pay yourself first (and put it in a savings account) before paying the rest of your bills, the amount in your savings account will grow so that you can invest it in mutual funds and an IRA.

♦ Deal with problems as they present themselves. The solution may only be temporary until you can devise a better one, but come to terms with what you are facing. If not, the problem will resurface again and again—sometimes twenty or thirty years later. It will cost you much less pain if you deal with problems in a timely manner.

♦ Creativity takes many forms. Set no limits.

♦ Sometimes the events occurring throughout the world can be overwhelming, and we wonder if we can really make a difference. The words of Charles Clements, "Each of us has to believe we can make a difference," have helped me realize that I can make a difference in someone's life, one person at a time. It is not my path in this life to create global changes, but that is okay. Helping one person at a time is just as good.

♦ Before adding another job to your life, disengage from a prior one. Balance. One can give too much to the community and lose oneself in the process—all in the name of good works.

♦ Smile at others, but most important, smile often to yourself. There will be times when you are alone, even within a great relationship, but you never need to be lonely.

♦ Treasure and nurture the wonderful gift that you are.

PAULA CATHY (PENKAVA) GOLDEN

M any years ago I was on a fellowship learning to be a teacher of family medicine. Little did I realize that in becoming a teacher I moved one step closer to becoming a healer. That two-year teaching fellowship taught me many things that I can begin to articulate only now.

Someone once said that everything has its own beauty, but not everyone sees it. I believe every person and situation that enters our lives is a teachable moment, but not everyone has the wisdom to see it. Use your innate wisdom to know that every situation and person that comes into your life is there to teach you something—even if it is unpleasant. Only when you live in this way can you grow and become the unique and special person that you were meant to be.

We are immersed in a time of great change. Some have referred to this as a "paradigm shift" that affects every aspect of our society. I believe we are experiencing a major shift in our way of thinking. This new paradigm has profound implications for your future, and it is important that you understand what this great change entails. When there is a change of this magnitude, our deep values as a people change. These deep values are really just the rules for living that are socialized into each one of us from birth on. I would like to share what I believe are the new deep values, and contrast them with the old. I think these will become our rules for living.

Living competitively versus living cooperatively. Living competitively is the deep value that many of us were given. It implies that you must constantly compete in life, and only by being better than everyone else can you be successful. It is in essence a never-ending treadmill, based on a scarcity mentality, and it leads only to separation, loneliness, and despair. This mentality makes you view all your fellow beings as competitors whom you must beat in the game of life.

Living cooperatively is the deep value that will be our future. Only through cooperation and sharing of ideas can we achieve our true potential as sentient beings. However, living cooperatively does not imply that you must compromise with others, although there will be times when that is necessary. Truly cooperative living is synergistic. It is two people coming together not to reach a compromise somewhere in the middle between their opposing views, but to devise a third option that neither individual had considered. Only when you truly respect others and their thoughts can you remain open to new possibilities. When relationships are truly synergistic, they combine the best of both people into a unique third option that neither had considered before their interaction. Remember, everyone who enters our lives has something to teach us, every day. Everyone has his or her own wisdom; have the wisdom to see it.

Predictability and uncertainty. We used to base our view of achievable reality on the notion that life is predictable. We designed our lives, families, and organizations to be as predictable and stable as possible. Some stability is necessary, but we all know life is not predictable or stable. Nature teaches us that the more stable a system is, the more likely it is to die. Life is about change, and adapting to change. Some stability is also desirable, for without it we would have chaos. But too much stability prevents creativity and adaptability, and it makes synergistic living impossible. Always strive to keep a dynamic balance between stability in your life and being open to the change that will inevitably occur.

Life is uncertain, and we must all become comfortable with this uncertainty. Only when life has an element of uncertainty can creativity and growth occur. Realize that uncertainty in your life is the raw material for you to grow and develop your unique qualities. Remember that every moment of your life is a teachable moment. Unpredictable moments offer the greatest opportunities for your uniqueness to emerge.

External and internal authority. External authority is another deep value many of us grew up with. We often believe that those around us are more knowledgeable than we are. Consequently, we defer to their wisdom or knowledge instead of our own. We have psychologists to tell us how to raise our children and how to have a happy marriage. We have physicians who tell us how we should live to be healthy. We have teachers who tell us how to learn. These subject-matter experts can provide useful information, but only you are an expert on yourself, and the only one qualified to decide how to use that information.

Internal authority is the emerging deep value that will serve you well in the future. Life is not a series of learning events, as we are sometimes led to believe. Life is really about remembering who we really are—our true spiritual nature and oneness with all things. We are born with this wisdom and need only rekindle its essence to have the information we need to live. I know your mother, and I am sure that one of her gifts to you is honoring your internal wisdom. I saw her safeguard it when you were little. It is now your responsibility to nurture and continue what your mother started. Honor others and the information they bring to you, but only you can decide how to use that information to your greatest good.

Individuality and relationship. Individuality is the essence of the old deep values. We are told to pull ourselves up by our bootstraps and never to rely on anyone else. That goes hand in hand with the concept of living competitively. We are taught that we come into this world alone and leave it alone, and anything we acquire is through our own efforts. Nothing could be further from the truth. We are never alone; we are always surrounded by love; we just don't always see it.

Honor all the uniqueness that is yours, but please understand that for you truly to develop your gifts requires entering into relationships with others.

Relationship is the foundation of the new deep values. We all start life dependent on our parents for physical, emotional, and spiritual survival. But eventually we achieve some form of independence and begin a journey toward individuality. Understand that there are many shades of individuality, and your individual essence will continue to grow throughout your life.

But there is a third stage of growth: interdependence. You must evolve from a state of dependence to independence, and ultimately to interdependence— the condition in which you depend on others, who also depend on you. True spiritual growth requires that you enter this state of being. The more you understand your own individuality and uniqueness, the more beneficial are the relationships you enter. The self is the essence of who you are, but it is redefined with every relationship. And when you reenter a relationship, you will sense that it has changed from what it was before. This is a cyclical process of immense potential. Only when you begin to understand this can you enter into true synergy with life. See yourself not as a being isolated in biological clothing, but as an energy field interacting with other energy fields. When you enter a relationship with another person without judging that person, and listen with your spirit, you create a portal that allows energy to flow between the two of you and connect you to the greater whole that is life.

The present moment. Living in the present moment is a requisite for true relationships. When you live out of your memory, you live in the past; when you live for the future, you are susceptible to anxiety and disappointment. Live in the present moment, not thinking too much about the past or being anxious about the future but seeing the present for what it really is. Whenever you enter a relationship with another person or event, be fully present. Don't recreate the person or event in front of you from past memories; that is doing both yourself and the other a disservice. When you process each moment through past memories or thoughts, you are really living mindlessly, because you develop a reliance on old patterns of thought. Learn to live mindfully, constantly creating new thought patterns. Treat even those you see every day as new relationships and discover them anew. Treat events and places the same way.

Remember the first time you met someone special—how alive your senses were and how special you felt? But over time, that specialness gradually fades because we begin living out of past memories, or living mindlessly. Always strive to be mindful and conscious of every interaction you have. Every time you enter a relationship mindfully, you not only enhance your own growth but also activate your body's natural healing ability. Our relationships and living in the present moment may be as close as we can get to a magic elixir of life.

Healing is truly an internal process. I became a better physician when I realized that I have no ability to heal anyone but myself. My role as a physician is to help others connect to and activate their natural healing ability. Understand that you have the ability to heal yourself. That ability is enhanced when you strive to be the truly unique and authentic person you were meant to be, and when you recognize that your relationships are potential sources of strength and healing. Honor yourself and your relationships: they are a powerful source of healing.

I have shared complex ideas with you. You must read them with your heart as well as your head for them to make any sense. Please understand that life is not about learning so much as it is about remembering who you truly are. Everything you will ever need is already inside you. Your job is to discover the wisdom that resides within.

TERRY GOLDEN, M.D.

There is something I learned from a friend many years ago that I'm pleased to pass on to you. If you already use the technique, good for you. I wish that I had learned it much earlier in my life. It really cuts down on stress.

My friend learned this while working toward his doctorate in behavior modification. There was a study done in elementary school classrooms where teachers complained that they had a disruptive student in the class. The teachers were instructed to count all disruptions that occurred for a specified period of time. The results were very interesting. In many cases, the students who were considered disruptive turned out to be no more so than many other students.

This was very helpful to me, because I knew that the only behavior I could control or change was my own. If the counting or annoying or disruptive behaviors proved that I was overreacting with little or no provocation, I had to change my behavior. If the number of incidents was high, I could confront the individual and perhaps we could work out a way to bring the number down to a level comfortable for both of us. Alternatively, I could remove myself from the environment.

Elizabeth Janeway wrote, "We older women who know we aren't heroines can offer our younger sisters, at the very least, an honest report of what we have learned and how we have grown."

May you continue to learn and grow your entire life. Embrace change in both body and mind and enjoy every minute of the good times. If and when the not-so-good times arrive, remember that they will not persist forever—nothing does. Remind yourself that without some not-so-good times, the really good times in life might not be so sweet.

My best wishes go with you into your future. I hope that you will accomplish whatever you set out to.

Please come have a cup of tea with me at the cottage. Maybe we will have steamed clams and chowder, too!

ARLOA CHRISTIANSEN-SAMBOL

Life can be hard, and any little hint to smooth the way is worth passing on. My best wishes to you for a healthy and happy life.

♦ Plants make a house a home. As much as some of us love cats or dogs, it's not always practical to have them. I have never heard of a place that stipulates "No plants allowed."

♦ Beware of your surroundings—keep safe and look up and around.

♦ Life is not always fair.

♦ Take a lot of pictures and keep a daily journal. It's amazing the things we forget.

♦ About money management: our family motto seems to be "Buy high—sell low," so I will not be giving any advice on this topic!

♦ Always follow the Golden Rule.

♦ No guts, no glory. Sometimes you have to take chances for the big rewards.

♦ Don't analyze everything to death. Some poems and stories should be enjoyed and have whatever meaning you decide they have. Robert Frost is one of my favorite poets, and "Stopping by Woods on a Snowy Evening" is one of my all-time favorite poems. I have heard this poem discussed and what each line "really" means. I enjoy the quiet calm of this poem—I don't need or want explanations—just the feeling of peace I get when reading it.

♦ Never be envious. There will always be others who are richer, smarter, prettier, thinner, taller, get the job you want, etc. You will literally make yourself miserable obsessing about them. Be happy with what you have and work to your highest potential—this is all you can ask of yourself and life.

♦ Save some of life's little treasures. Years from now it will be interesting for you to look back on your writings, art work, and even an extra-hard math test! As a parent, I've saved a sampling of each child's papers and drawings. My parents, although proud of my accomplishments at the moment, never kept my childhood papers or artwork. I feel a sense of loss because of it. A watercolor instructor once told me that all paintings should be kept and reviewed from time to time. In this way advancement can be chronicled. If you ever get discouraged, look back at your first efforts and see just how far you've come.

I'm a firm believer in volunteering. (I must admit I've been fortunate not to have to work outside the home, and to have the luxury of time to volunteer.) The great thing about most volunteer jobs is you can choose your days and hours of work—it's flexible and can be bent to your schedule. Even if you have a few hours a year, there will be a volunteer position for you! How about a "hugger" at the Special Olympics?

I have been married to my best friend for thirty years. We moved seventeen times in twenty years thanks to the military. During all the moves and upheaval, we had three wonderful children. As with any marriage, we've had ups and downs, but when the dust settles we are always together.

My husband, Joe, always teases me about being a cheap date. Because I'm able to appreciate every small statement of love, my world is full of loving surprises. Joe walks through a small park on the way to the hospital parking garage. In the fall, he often picks the most brilliant leaf he can reach and gives it to me when he arrives home. I love these little jewel-toned gifts—wonderful reminders of the colorful northeast autumns of my childhood.

Joe often calls me to a window or outside to see the moonrise, sunset, a covey of quail, or one of the roses in full bloom, or how many blossoms are on the apple tree. I don't tell him I was working in the garden all morning and know about the rose or apple blossoms. I enjoy his enthusiasm and make plans for the rest of the growing season as we walk around the yard. Lest you get the wrong impression—I have a black thumb—so *anything* that manages to grow under my care is considered a miracle!

I thank God daily for the wonderful parents and childhood I enjoyed. My mother, Beatrice, is my role model. Sadly, my mother died ten weeks after our first-born arrived. She was so very proud to be a grandmother. I will always remember the love, security and laughter she brought into so many lives—and it will always make me sad that my children never got to know her.

Our three children are fun to be around and are interesting people. There are five to six years between each kid. At one time, we had one in kindergarten, one in sixth grade, and a senior in high school. We almost lived at the various schools between concerts, games, meetings, and volunteering.

Take a lot of pictures of your children and life in general. It's amazing how we forget things over the years. It's important for children to be able to look back and see what things were like when they were growing up. There was the winter our four-year-old decided she was tired of waiting to go swimming so she wore knee socks, a sweatshirt, and her bathing suit over the shirt. Or, the time when little brother decided to help peel cucumbers. Or the bedraggled, three-generation canoe trip in Alaska—Grandfather, father, and oldest son. Every picture is a gem in our family picture treasure chest.

Write down cute things your children say and keep what they write—"My heart is broken forever. I will never speak to you again. Love, Rebecca." And to think we were thrilled when she learned to write. "Don't be upset Mom, my unit is being sent to Desert Storm." This note from my son ranked right up there with my spouse telling me that he, too, had orders for Desert Storm.

Movers had been packing our household for two days and the van was due the next morning. The three-year-old, of cucumber fame, unpacked all the boxes in his room. When we asked why, "The man tried to steal all my toys and books!" was the reply.

Some happy moments, some sad, but all the fabric of our family's life.

LINDA SANKER

To save a few bucks and to salve my environmentally concerned conscience, I drive to a "Park and Ride" where I catch a bus to work. Lately it's become harder and harder for me to meet the bus's schedule. I fly out of the house, race down the street, and hope against hope that the bus will be running late so that I'll be able to beat it to the "Park and Ride."

One such morning I slammed my parked car's door closed just as the bus pulled up to the stop. I really had to dash to join the queue formed to board the bus. It was only with my peripheral vision that I noticed someone walking across the parking lot. It was a young man who was walking using crutches attached to arm braces. I was preoccupied with myself, so I barely registered his presence until I heard a collective gasp from the rest of the bus passengers. Then I looked up and focused on the outside world. As I looked out the window, I heard someone say, "He's trying to catch the bus." It was a wet morning, and a stunned silence ensued as the driver pulled out into the traffic. I looked back to see that the young man was struggling alone to get to his feet where he had fallen on the wet pavement.

In a perfect world, someone (preferably myself) would have stood up and shouted, "Stop the bus, that man needs help!" Was the bus driver a heartless wretch to pull away? Was he more interested in staying on schedule than in helping another human being? Did the driver even realize that something unusual had happened? Was the man even trying to catch this bus? Didn't anyone on the bus have the courage of his or her convictions? How could I have been so self-involved that I didn't notice what was happening? Was this a test? Did all the passengers riding Bus 9 into the city at 7:26 that morning fail the test miserably? Is there a lesson here?

I've noticed, as I get older and my life's path gets longer, that I have many more questions than answers. I choose to believe that this is a good thing. Ask questions; ask lots and lots of questions. And furthermore, question the answers that you get to those questions. I've noticed that the answers keep changing, and I want to know why.

Since I do not have the answers for this particular set of questions, in this particular situation, I choose to interpret it as a wake-up call for me. "Pay attention—pay attention to life!" a larger voice is saying. "There is much to be done, and you can do it better. Appreciate each moment, each phase, each question, each color, each sound, each smell, each noise, each smile, each frown, each happy and healthy day. Somewhere and sometime, all that you have noticed, absorbed, and appreciated will add up to the answers you need for your own truth."

ANNETTE YOUNG

As your responsibilities grow and the excitement of life sweeps you in, you might not have the time to consider all the information you have received. As a matter of fact, you will be creating your own information. As a way to express thoughts important to me, I have chosen to mention some of the highs and lows of my life.

As you are wrapped up in youth, peer pressure is very important. You need your friends, and they need you! They are an asset. You are all molding and helping one another to develop. I had friends that I looked up to, trusted, and followed for several years. Today some of them are still friends. Others have been lost to drugs and alcohol or lifestyles unacceptable to me at my present stage of growth.

Life is about choices. You will make them every day until you draw your final breath. Choose wisely; be aware that there is a choice. So many things are just "done." You may think about them later and say, "It's just something that I do"—not even realizing that at some point in the past, you chose to do it. Don't hesitate to make a choice, though; making the wrong choice and then realizing it is how you learn. The true measure of character is recognizing right and wrong and reacting to the decision you have made.

When I was young I used to think that people older than me had been frozen in a "time zone." Now that I am older, I have realized that people who cast themselves in a mold restrict their ability to be creative. For example, someone might say, "I would never wear a tie," or "I always wear a hat," or "I would never do that." What is the big deal? Are their personalities so restricted or shallow that if they did something different, they would become a different person?

I'm sure you've heard the saying, "Don't be afraid of new ideas." I would like to add, "Don't be afraid of old ideas." Family values, morals, and lifestyle choices can all be rewarding by building modern traditions with proven building materials.

The greatest gift you have is your mind. Everyone knows you are smart, but learn to use your mind. The more you push your boundaries, the farther you will go. When I was in school, I didn't like math, and I wasn't good at it; yet today, a large part of my work is accounting. As a young person I had all kinds of restrictions on what I could do. But today I know that it takes a challenge, and someone to believe you can meet it, to expand your abilities. Push to achieve the greatness you deserve.

Let me tell you about a recent event in my life. I got married! I waited a long time. Everyone else I knew was married. I guess I wasn't willing to compromise: I married for love, not out of loneliness. I lived many years of my life alone, but as a result, I got to know myself and learned to accept myself and make changes I thought were necessary. It made me a better person and a better husband.

One point I would make is *that life is precious*. You must be aware of this as a young woman. The "gift of life" is just that: a gift from God. Once in my life I was given a daughter. I did not know she was coming. I did not know when she was born. I did not know of her existence until she was nine months old. She was so perfect! Then, when she was eleven months old, her mother moved. I saw and heard nothing of my daughter until she was eleven years old. I missed seeing her grow up. An argument could be made that I was not ready to be a "dad." But I was never given the choice.

It was difficult at first to establish a relationship with my daughter. You have to prove you're trustworthy when you start in the middle. But as time went on, we became comfortable, and over a longer period we grew closer to each other. My daughter is one of the greatest gifts in my life. She has given me hope when I was hopeless and inspiration when I had none. In all truth, she has given me life. When I was in the depths of despair and my world had caved in around me, she was there. At fourteen, she gave me a reason to want to continue.

Sometimes it is not convenient to have a child, but the rewards are immeasurable. If you ignore all that has been presented to you in this book, *please,*

please recognize the value of life. Having a child is the ultimate consequence for your actions. Choose your partner carefully. You will be linked with that person your entire life.

ROYCE YOUNG

Laugh often. Try not to take yourself so seriously. Life is too short.

Be flexible. It is the best way to deal with life's ups and downs.

Cherish your friendships. Value each one, for each is unique and special.

Growth is painful. Setbacks and failures are necessary to achieve competence.

Develop life skills necessary for being independent.

Never forget the value of the simple things in life—a week in the woods, or appreciating a beautiful day.

Giving of yourself feels good.

A positive self-image is necessary to succeed.

Strive for a balance between work, leisure, and family.

As bad as things may seem during a crisis, it will get better.

LISA SNELLA

What words would I have for a young adult just starting out? I think life is all about love: love for ourselves, and love for others.

To live a rewarding life, it is imperative that we love ourselves. We have the capacity to generate the love for ourselves that we may sadly seek only in others. When our focus is always out there, outside ourselves, seeking someone else's love and approval, we lose our opportunity to be who we are. We settle for fashioning ourselves to suit someone else, and in time we come to resent them for it. We do not have to give up pieces of ourselves to be loved by others! Our mission in life is to embrace ourselves, to accept who we are, to explore our interests and talents, and to speak our truths. With this acceptance, we are able to fashion our lives in a way that honors and nurtures us. We are able to take responsibility for our lives, our choices, and not give our power to someone else.

In times of trouble, we need to show ourselves the love and mercy that we more easily show others. By becoming our own best allies, we are able to let go of blame and judgment. We are able to acknowledge the truth of our hearts, and stand by ourselves until we are able to gather enough clarity and perspective to move on. Even in times of trouble, we always have a choice. We make better choices when we feel compassion for our journey and ourselves.

Life requires constant contemplation. Someone once said that an unexamined life wasn't worth living. It is easy to get off track, or just sit back and react to what life throws our way. A happier life is one in which we give ourselves time: time to think, time to be, time to chart our course anew. Giving ourselves time is an act of love, and it helps us live with intention.

It is perhaps a cliché, but I do feel that the Golden Rule provides the best guide to loving relationships with others. "Do unto others what you would have them do unto you" allows us the benefit of kindness, compassion, and forgiveness. No one wants to be told how to live, what to do, what to feel, how to be. It is not an easy charge, particularly if we are not happy with our lives and ourselves. If we have not learned how to love ourselves first and have not taken responsibility for our own lives, we will be needy and will want to direct those around us to do the things that will make us feel more loved, more valued, more whole.

I believe Abraham Lincoln's dictum, "Most people are about as happy as they make their minds up to be." Our happiness, in the end, is our responsibility. True, there is much that others may contribute to our happiness, but life is unpredictable. Those who are here today may not be tomorrow. In the end, all any person has is herself.

I recently read a prayer that reflects my thoughts on our responsibility to show love to those we don't know:

May God bless you with discomfort
At easy answers, half-truths, and
Superficial relationships, so that
You will live deep in your heart.

May God bless you with anger at
Injustice, oppression, and
Exploitation of people and the earth
So that you will work for justice,
Equity, and peace.

May God bless you with tears to
Shed for those who suffer so you will
Reach out your hands to comfort
Them and change their pain into joy.

And may God bless you with
The foolishness to think that you
Can make a difference in the world,
So you will do the things which
Others say cannot be done.

—Source unknown [distributed by School
of the America Watch Northwest]

Reaching out to help others is all about the circle of love: when the giving is the receiving, and the receiving is the giving. When we live "deep in our hearts" and use our God-given talents to help others, we receive so much in return! We must put our lives where our values are. Working to share our talents with others is good for our souls and for our community—the family of man. When we help others, our view of the world is expanded and enriched, as is our capacity to love. We learn things beyond the range of our day-to-day existence. We gain insight and compassion for the difficult lives some must lead, the hardships they must endure. We are given the blessing of seeing the strength of the human spirit, and its capacity for courage and perseverance.

It's all about love, in the end. Fill your life with love, for yourself and others, and you will have no regrets. I send love for the journey.

DARLENE FLACK

Y ou have grown from being children and are now embarking on an exciting journey into adulthood. You have unfolded gradually, as a flower from a bud, into people of great possibilities. Your interest and involvement in games contributed to what you are today. These contests were more than a means to occupy your time. You learned many lessons from sports, board games, and cards. I have watched each of you deeply engrossed in various games. You competed very capably at these games. They contributed to your vocabulary skills and helped you learn to employ strategy.

My sons learned many valuable lessons from sports, too. Like you, they were involved in summer ball leagues at an early age—T-ball, Little League, and Babe Ruth. Yes, they learned and developed from being on the ball field. From being team members they learned sportsmanship and how to get along with others, but they also received much wise instruction from people in the stands.

Soon you will have the opportunity to make all your own decisions. There are choices that you must make. I would like to impart one bit of wisdom my boys learned from the baseball stands that may be helpful to you. They would hear shouts of "Make it be there!" This is a phrase about commitment. In baseball terms, it means you commit to swing at the ball only when it passes over the plate in your favored zone. You have great opportunities ahead of you. When you can pick and choose the people, ideas, and objects in your life, just as in baseball, choose to swing only at the balls that are in the right zone.

Most parents agree that summer league ball has an important influence on American youth. Throughout the United States, in every community, boys and girls try very hard to win. They practice and psych themselves up for the game. My sons were intent about their games, as you were. The game was always on their minds. I can still hear them saying, "Dad, throw me some pitches!" or "Dad, hit me some balls!"

My sons knew I was supporting them by attending their games with fellow parents. Your parents gave you that support also. You will need to feel support at times, even after you leave for college. There really is someone in the stands cheering for you. Seek Him out and reach out to Him. He is always there available for you.

The team's parents cheered when a team member made a play in the field. It was exciting to see a player of the opposing team put out at first or at home. We yelled our encouragement when our team was at bat. As you know, the batter stands all alone at the plate. There is no one to block for her. She will hit, or she will strike out. She needs much encouragement. There will be times when you, too, will be lonely and will need encouragement. Seek out those who will help you to be the best you can be and who will stand with you when the going is rough.

My sons would come to the plate. They would be anxious. They would want too much to get a hit. Sometimes they would swing at the first pitch. The expectancy and desire was too great for them not to swing. Sometimes after they swung, they would realize the ball was out of their reach and they should have let it go by. When the batter swung and missed the first pitch, the stands would erupt with shouts of instruction: "Make it be there!" "Look 'em over, kid!" "Wait for your pitch!"

You will soon be standing in the batter's box of life. You will be making choices and involving yourself with others. As you do, remember your baseball days. Ask yourself, "Is it all there?" When you are choosing friends, your life's mate, a career, investments, or purchases, don't swing until all that you desire is there.

BOB BARRETT

To order additional copies of

Essays from the Heart

Book: $12.95   Shipping/Handling: $3.50

Contact: ***BookPartners, Inc.***
P.O. Box 922
Wilsonville, OR 97070

E-mail: bpbooks@teleport.com
Fax: 503-682-8684
Phone: 503-682-9821
Order: 1-800-895-7323

Visit our Web site at:
www.bookpartners.com